Main Entrance Regent's Park Buildings 1913–1941.

Main Entrance Regent's Park Buildings 1950–1985.

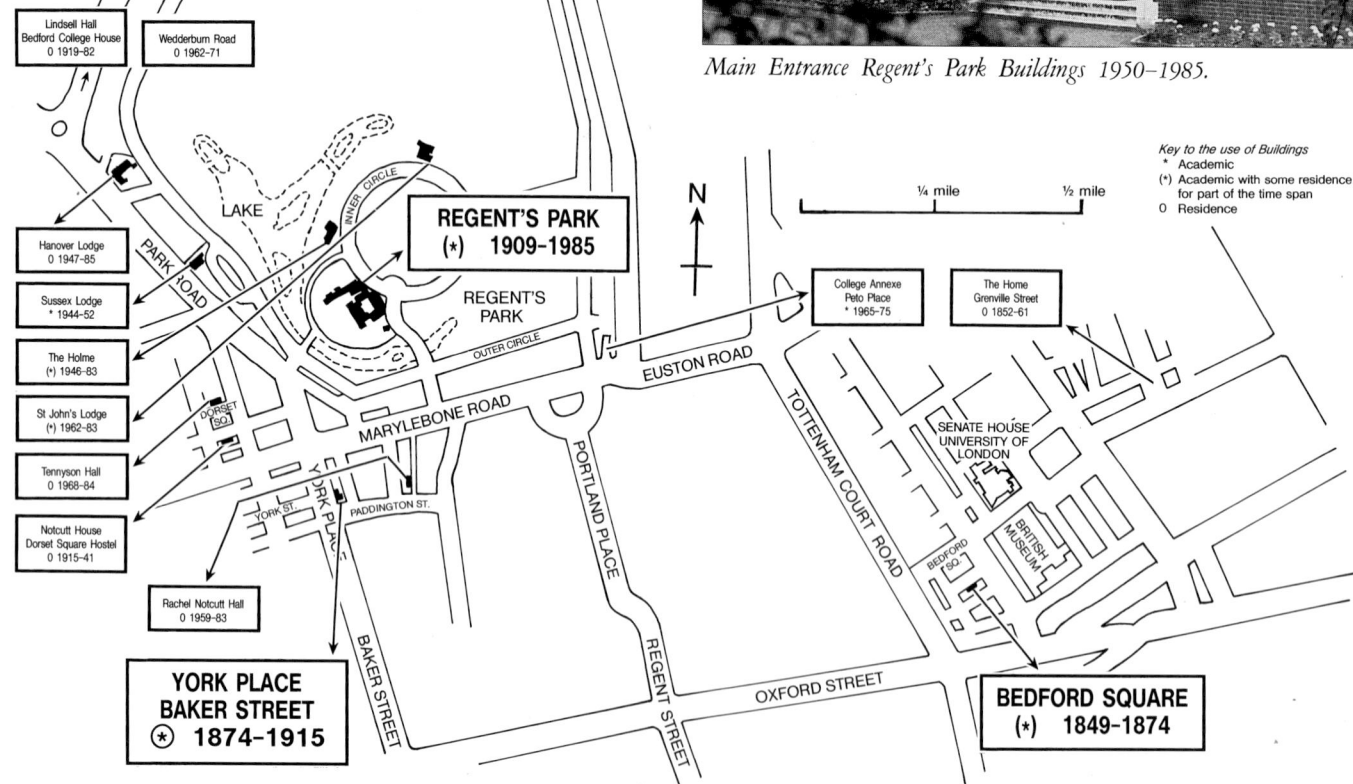

7, 8, 9 York Place, Baker Street.

47 and 48 Bedford Square, the two houses next to the white house.

EDUCATING WOMEN

A Pictorial History of
BEDFORD COLLEGE
University of London
1849–1985

A photographic record of Bedford College covering 136 years from 1849 to 1985. During this time the College was in central London and it was part of the federal University of London from the start of that institution in 1900.

compiled and written by
Linna Bentley

THIS BOOK grew out of the exhibition presented at the last Reunion in the College in 1985. It owes much to the people who came that day and to those who have since sent to us their photographs and mementoes to keep or copy for the College archives.

THE AUTHOR, Dr Linna Bentley, was on the staff of the Department of Botany in Bedford College from 1952 to 1985.

CONTENTS

1 **FOREWORD**
by Dame Marjorie Williamson

2 **INTRODUCTION, SUBJECTS TAUGHT**
Principals and the Arms

4 **PLANS FOR THE COLLEGE IN BEDFORD SQ**
Need, Means, Aims, Preparations

6 **EARLY DAYS AND WOMEN WITH INFLUENCE**
Staff, Boarding House, Lady Visitors

8 **STUDENTS, STAFF AND COUNCIL 1860s**
A Resident, Staff, Professors, Councillors

10 **THE REID TRUST, WOMEN WITH POWER**
E Bostock, J Martineau, E Smith, R Notcutt

12 **YORK PLACE, BAKER STREET, 1874**
Managers, Art School, Magazine, Boating

14 **THE SHAEN WING 1890**
Royal Opening, Laboratories, Residence

16 **COLLEGE WOMEN OF THE 1890s**
E Penrose, C Raisin, H Busk, Greek Plays

18 **STUDENT FUNDING. YORK PLACE LIBRARY**
Numbers, Scholarships, Grants, Bookplate

20 **COMMUNITY AND SOCIAL LIFE IN YORK PLACE**
BCSA, Colours, Gymnasium, Residence

22 **50 YEARS OF ACADEMIC PROGRESS**
Departments, Letters, Intercollegiates

24 **JUBILEE CELEBRATIONS 1899**
Conference, Conversazione, Garden Party

26 **TIMETABLES**
1849, 1879, 1898, 1903

28 **A CHARTER AND AN APPEAL 1903-1909**
Angel Gabriel, Electra, Staff of 1903

30 **GRADUATION AND A NEW SITE 1903-1911**
Presentation Days, Songs, South Villa

32 **REGENT'S PARK 1911-1913**
Plans, Objections, Buildings

34 **ROYAL PATRONAGE AND COLLEGE PRIDE**
Former Students of Distinction

36 **LIBRARY AND LECTURE ROOMS 1914**
Tate, Wernher, Sundial, The Large, Science

38 **SCIENCE COURSES 1914**
Laboratories, Museum, Experiments, Training

40 **OLIVER DINING HALL AND COMMON ROOMS 1915**
Dining and Social Traditions, Relaxations

42 **RESIDENCE, THE STUDENT UNION 1917**
Study-bedrooms, Union Committee, Gate Lodge

44 **THE ACADEMIC WOMAN, WORLD WAR ONE**
Caroline Spurgeon, Graduation, War Work

46 **SPACE FOR SPORT 1917-1922**
The Grounds and the Park Lake

48 **POST-WAR INCREASE IN NUMBERS 1920-1926**
Overcrowding, Ex-army Huts, Academics

50 **A WIDER RANGE OF ACTIVITIES 1920-1926**
Nursing, Field Work, BCA, Boating Skirts

52 **UNIONS AND UNIFORM 1920s**
BCAU, ULU, Colours, Dress, Song, Poem

54 **RAISING FUNDS 1919-1927**
The Need, Theatre, The Foundation Stone

56 **THE TUKE BUILDING 1930**
Building, Funds, Observatory, Opening

58 **THE EARLY 1930s**
Busk Gates, M Miles, Tuke Hall, Library

60 **THE MID 1930s**
Women Staff, Boating, Technicians

62 **THE LATE 1930s AND EVACUATION**
Roberts, Reunion, Commemoration, Cambridge

64 **LONDON AND THE BOMBING 1941**
Tenants, Fire-fighting, Ruins, NUS

66 **RETURNING 1944-1946**
New Space, Colours, Magazines, Male Students

68 **RECONSTRUCTION 1947, 1948 and 1949**
Re-naming Buildings, Oliver, Centenary

70 **CENTENARY 1949, HERRINGHAM 1951**
Celebrations, Use of Space, Societies

72 **CELEBRATIONS AND SCHOLARSHIP 1952**
Darwin, Completion, Lilian Penson, Academics

74 **THE 1950s**
Space, Supporting Staff, Students, Telescope

76 **ROBBINS AND MEN 1963-1967**
Expansion, Changes, Male Undergraduates

78 **SCR AND FELLOWS 1965-1969**
Prefabs, The Holme, K Lonsdale, Refectory

80 **HANOVER LODGE AND TENNYSON HALL**
Residences, The Garden Gate

82 **LINDSELL HALL. DEGREES AWARDED**
Bedford College House, Qualifications

84 **THE 1970s**
Protest, E E Humphrey, Sport, Development

86 **THE LAST TEN YEARS**
Students, Final Appeal, Finance, Merger

88 **REUNION AND FAREWELL 1985**
Last Session, Final Reunion

90 **MOVING AND END WORD**
End Word by Professor Dorothy Wedderburn

DATA

2 Principals of Bedford College 1893-1985

3 Subjects Taught and Practised 1849-1985

18 Numbers of Students 1850-1984

19 Funding of Students 1854-1984

77 Percentage of Male Students 1966-1985

81 Residences 1852-1985

83 London Degrees Awarded 1881-1984

© 1991 Linna Bentley. All rights reserved.
Published by Alma Publishers, Surrey ISBN 0 9517497 0 6, in conjunction with Royal Holloway and Bedford New College, University of London, ISBN 0 900145 81 1

FOREWORD

It was a pleasure to be asked to write a Foreword to this Pictorial History so lovingly compiled by Linna Bentley. It tells, more vividly than many words could do, the story of Bedford College from its beginning in 1849 through growth and change until 1985 when it ceased to be a separate entity within the University of London.

Bedford College has its place in history as the first institution established specifically for the higher education of women, twenty years before the foundation of the first of the women's colleges in Oxford or Cambridge. This it owes, to quote Dame Margaret Tuke, 'to the vision and faith of one woman, Elisabeth Jesser Reid'.

It is now partnered appropriately with another college of the University of London, established by its Founder Thomas Holloway, in 1886, for the same purpose 'that academic honours should be open to ladies in this College'.

Times have changed. It is now taken for granted that a girl has opportunities equal to those open to her brother and both of these one-time women's colleges have opened their doors to men. Here is a valuable record of days gone by. It will delight past students and old friends and will recall many varied memories.

To the College in its new incarnation as Royal Holloway and Bedford New College, Hail and Farewell.

Marjorie Williamson DBE
Lecturer in Physics at Bedford College 1945–1955
Principal of Royal Holloway College 1962–1973

Tuke Building.

THE ARMS OF THE COLLEGE

Argent between two Flaunches paly bendy Or and Sable a Cross partée throughout Gules voided of the field, surmounted by an open Book of the second, on a Chief of the third an Antique Lamp Gold inflamed proper.

The grant of arms was made to the College in September 1913. The arms embody emblems of the Danish Royal family and the Teck family, sanction for the use of these being graciously given by Their Majesties Queen Alexandra and Queen Mary. The representatives of the late Miss Bostock allowed the use of her motto 'Esse quam videri', thus linking her memory with the College arms.

PRINCIPALS OF BEDFORD COLLEGE

1893–1898   EMILY PENROSE MA Oxon
            later – Principal of Royal Holloway College 1898–1907
            Principal of Somerville College, Oxford, 1907–1926 created DBE 1927, died 1942 aged 84 years

1898–1906   ETHEL HURLBATT MA Dublin
            later – Warden, Royal Victoria College, McGill Univ Montreal died 1934 aged 68 years

1907–1929   MARGARET J TUKE MA Cantab, MA Dublin
            created DBE 1932, died 1947 aged 84 years

1930–1951   GERALDINE E M JEBB MA Cantab
            created CBE 1952, died 1959 aged 73 years

1951–1964   NORAH L PENSTON BA DPhil Oxon
            died 1974 aged 70 years

1964–1971   ELIZABETH M CHILVER MA Oxon

1971–1981   JOHN N BLACK MA DPhil Oxon, DSc Adel

1981–1985   DOROTHY E WEDDERBURN MA Cantab
            Principal of Bedford College until the merger with Royal Holloway College on 1st August, 1985, and from then until 1990 Principal of the Royal Holloway and Bedford New College, University of London, situated at Egham in Surrey.

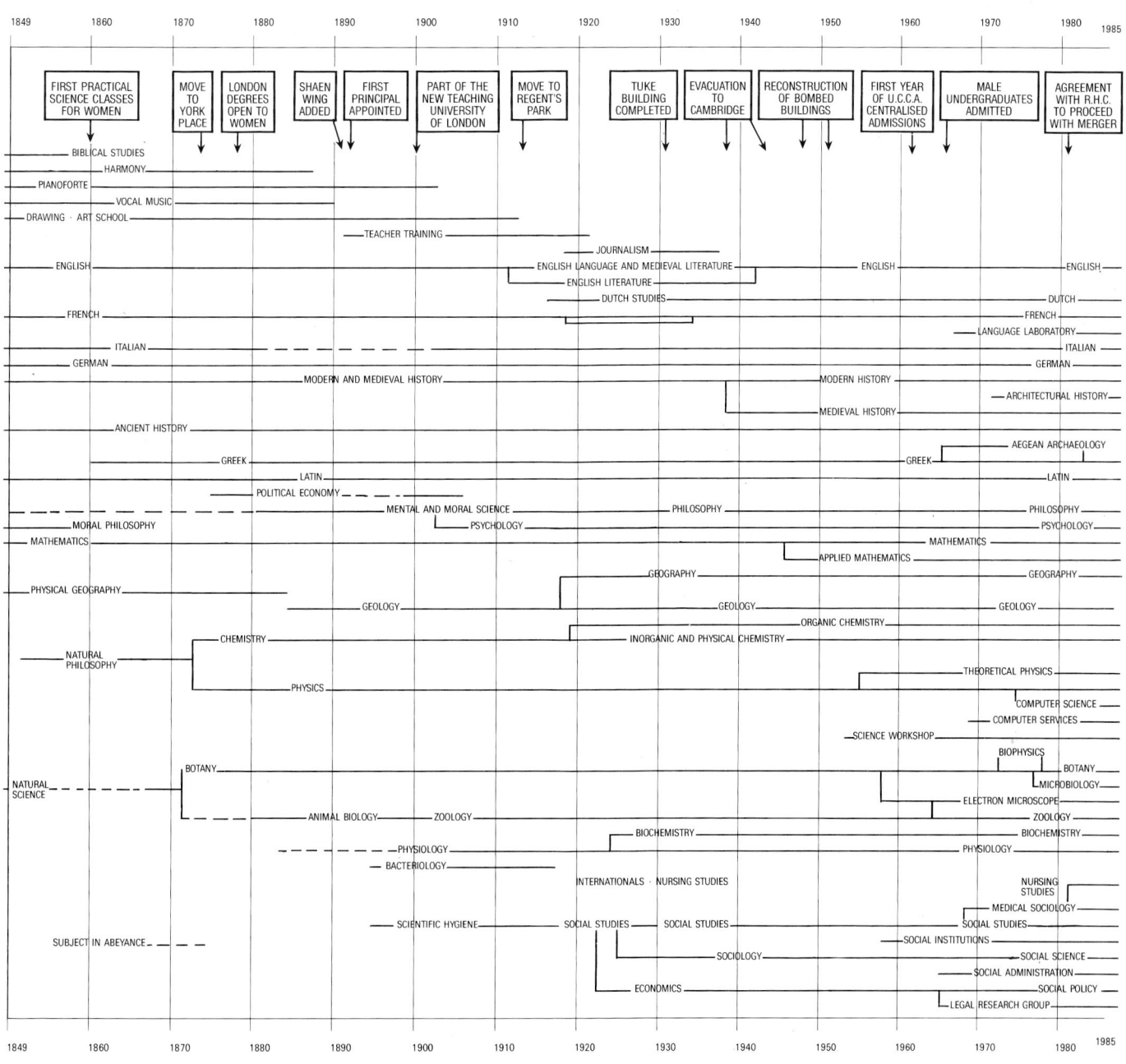

INTRODUCTION

Students were taught at Bedford College from the beginning of October, 1849 to July, 1985. A higher education, beyond that of schools, liberal in nature with a good choice of subjects and of university standard, was offered throughout these 136 years. The teaching in the early years was done entirely by men but from 1880 both men and women were involved in the teaching and research. The students – the undergraduates – were all women until 1965 and from then on there were approximately equal numbers of men and women.

In the schema above, a recurring theme is an increase in the range of subjects available in the College. The research activities of the scholars who did the teaching are echoed in the extending range of subjects offered to students. This extending range and complexity of teaching, given mainly within the college walls, is one factor which determined the nature of Bedford College.

At a number of stages in its history, those responsible for the College considered possible actions which, if taken, would have given us a very different college. The possibilities have included moving away from central London, restricting the range of subjects taught, enhancing the intercollegiate cooperation and ceasing or continuing to be a women's college. These and similar decisions, and the constraints within which they were taken, lay behind the story we have to tell.

The following pages reflect the achievements of those who worked within the College and the changing educational and social lives of the Bedford students throughout their 136 years in London and its University.

EDUCATING WOMEN

PLANS FOR THE COLLEGE IN BEDFORD SQUARE

There were to be no fanfares at the opening of Bedford College. In the summer of 1849 a simple prospectus was issued for a 'Ladies College in Bedford Square' offering advanced educational classes for women to be started in the October of that year. Seventeen subjects were listed together with the names of the men who would teach them. These were mainly professors employed also at other Colleges. Women would be admitted to the classes on payment of the fee and production of a reference. It was the object of the institution 'to provide for ladies, at a moderate expense', a University programme of lectures, examinations and exercises.

The Need

The prospectus was issued by a group of people who were convinced of the need for such a College. At this time boys but not girls could easily find an academic education beyond the level provided by school or a governess at home. Universities and Colleges were available for boys, who paid fees or were supported by scholarships. Life and work at a College stimulated the minds of young men from affluent families and also trained them for the professions. Meanwhile, their sisters stayed at home and dutifully prepared for marriage by practising domestic and social skills or maybe polished these same skills in a finishing school. Only very rarely did a determined daughter persuade her family to let her use books and open up for herself the intellectual world through subjects such as Latin, Greek, mathematics and history. It had not always been so but in the early years of the reign of Queen Victoria was the accepted pattern; this the 'Ladies College' hoped to change.

The Means

The motivation and the means for the founding of the College were provided by Elisabeth Reid, née Sturch, 1789–1866, who came from a strongly liberal and Unitarian background. She had inherited money on her early widowhood and again on the death of her parents which allowed her to travel, to support philanthropic causes and to develop a wide circle of well-educated friends. Mrs Reid's views on the need for better education for women gained practical shape during discussion with these friends. In 1849, when she was sixty years old, she went ahead with her plans and founded the College. She placed £1,500 with three male Trustees and persuaded some of her friends to serve on the management committees and others to act as teaching professors. They leased a house on the south side of Bedford Square which, as stated in the prospectus, was 'chosen as a suitable situation, from its being in the centre of a populous and wealthy neighbourhood, where such advantages as this College affords will be particularly valued'. The College took its name from the Square and retained this name-connection throughout its subsequent moves.

The Aims

As shown by Margaret Tuke in her 'History of Bedford College for Women, 1849-1937', the plans for the College were that it should be first, the provider of a liberal education for women, widening their outlook and developing their minds, second, non-sectarian but not anti-religious, having the highest aims for moral and spiritual life and third, that it should have women amongst its governors. In each of these aims it differed fundamentally from the other institutions in London which then offered education to women beyond that available in schools.

Other Institutions

In 1842, seven years before the start of the 'Ladies College', the first students entered the Whitelands Training Institution for Schoolmistresses in King's Road, Chelsea. The genesis and funding of this Institution came from the Church of England which, by means of 'The National Society for Promoting the Education of the Poor in the Principles of the Established Church', was responsible for the administration of the 'National' Schools. By 1849 Whitelands had sent forth in to the National Schools of the country, 146 certificated schoolmistresses, many of them Head Teachers, who were reported on by both Government and Church authorities in glowing terms. We do not know whether Mrs Reid was aware of Whitelands College; its connection with the National Society might distance it from her own Unitarian ideas, whilst its control by men and its emphasis on training for a specific job might have reinforced her own aims to provide a College which avoided both of these.

A movement began in 1845 from the Governesses Benevolent Institution which led to the founding of Queen's College opened in Harley Street in 1848. Queen's College was supported by the clergy of the Church of England, ruled by a Committee of men and intended for raising the standard of education of governesses. However, the founding and success of Queen's College appeared to be a stimulus to the ideas of Mrs Reid and her friends, some of whom were actively involved with Queen's College. The prospectus for the 'Ladies College in Bedford Square' acknowledges its near neighbour and states 'The success of this Institution proves that its founders rightly estimated the demand for a better and more extended system of female education than any which had previously been accessible'. The spirit is not of competition but of widening the educational opportunities for women.

The College's First House in Bedford Square.

Mrs Elisabeth Jesser Reid.

PLANS FOR THE COLLEGE IN BEDFORD SQUARE

James Booth.

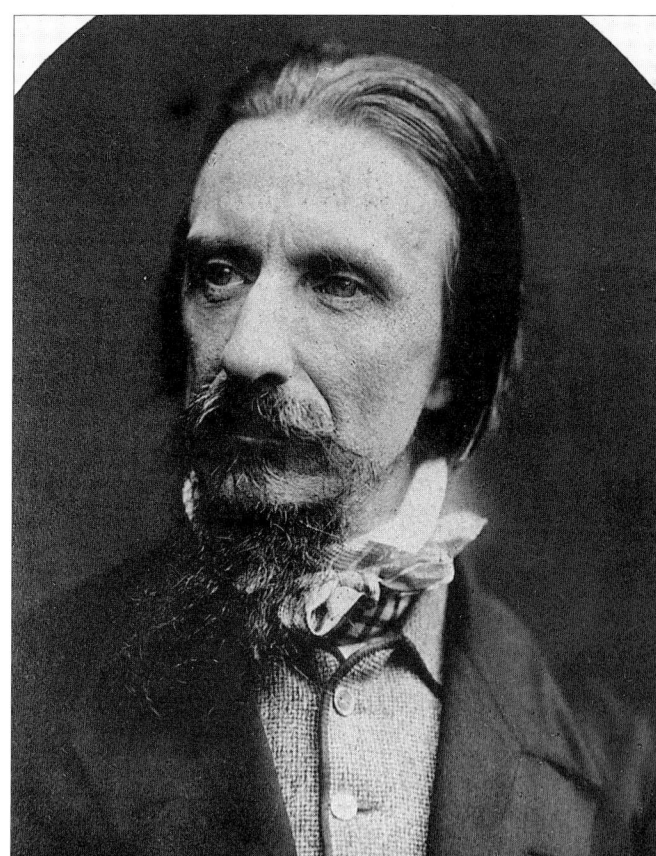
Francis Newman.

The Preparations

In 1849 committees were busy making preparations. Their meetings led to the agreed Prospectus, the furnishing of the house, the appointment of the Lady Visitors to act as mentors to the students, the appointment of seven more professors to join the four already in office and, finally, the preparation of a constitution for the management of the College. Although these meetings achieved a great deal they appear to have shown up the lack of committee experience of the women. Many of the ladies had no knowledge of committee discipline and some of them were slow to learn. This was particularly noticeable to the male professors with whom the women were meant to work on the General Committee but it was also apparent in their own, initially far more important, Committee of Ladies. The problem certainly influenced the constitution of the permanent committees.

The Ladies College was a venture with very little money and no purpose-built premises. It did not initially have any royal connections and was not allied to the main establishment of the day. As it held so few advantages it had to be extra careful of its reputation. The people who organised the College were well aware that if it appeared too strongly linked with religious dissent, whether non-conformist or free-thinking, it would not get sufficient students and fee income. The same would be true if it did not look to the decorum of the young ladies in its charge. These were the obvious risks for the College in the pursuit of its aims and to avoid them skilful preparations were necessary.

Two Early Stalwarts

Two men who were deeply involved in the preparations but who had left the College within two years of its opening were Francis Newman and James Booth.

Francis William Newman was Professor of Latin at University College, London, and formerly a Fellow of Balliol College, Oxford. He was a writer on religious subjects and on political, social and educational problems; he was the younger brother of the more famous John Henry, the future Cardinal. Francis Newman was a stalwart of the early years of the College, closely and actively involved in the planning and preparations, always ready with advice from his wide experience, he took on many administrative jobs. He was the Honorary Secretary to the first Council and the Board as well as the Professor of Ancient History and of Mental and Moral Science together with Political Economy. In 1851 he resigned from his professorship, his seat on Council and all his connections with the College amidst very difficult controversies concerned with the manner used to appoint teaching staff when trying to maintain the non-sectarian character of the College.

In 1953, in reply to the toast of *The College*, the then Professor of Geology, Leonard Hawkes, said 'The founders of Bedford College were unorthodox and advanced people of their time – men and women of the future – who emancipated themselves from the fetters of tradition. The man who did most for the infant College was a member of the famous Newman family – not the Cardinal who would not have lifted a finger for it, but his brother Francis, a scholar and a man of very different stamp'.

The Rev Dr James Booth FRS was also much involved in the committees that made the preparations. He was the Professor who taught physical geography and later mathematics. Fellow councillors elected him to be the first Chairman of the Council 1849–50. He helped with administration and was the Treasurer and looked after the details of the accounts until, after Council changed the accounting procedures, he resigned in December, 1850.

EDUCATING WOMEN

EARLY DAYS AND WOMEN WITH INFLUENCE

Early Days

Students appeared, classes were formed and teaching started for the Michaelmas Term in 1849. Now that the College was underway, its management took shape according to the proposed constitution. Men and women learnt the very new art of working together on the main executive and representative body to be called the Council. It was limited to nine members, five men and four women, three men being employed as Professors and three women being representatives of the Lady Visitors. The women retained considerable power, having final authority for 'all matters in which female propriety and comfort is concerned'. Above the Council was the Board which was the guardian of the constitution of the College. At this stage the constitution of the College was simply operated it was not formally adopted by the Board.

In the first year or so there were many changes. Some of the teaching Professors departed because of the low standard of the students on entry, some for other reasons, and replacements had to be found. In 1853 a school was started in the premises by Mrs Reid to help overcome the lack of proper schooling for girls and to provide students of much better standard to enter the College classes. A few of the students became resident, first in a house in Grenville Street and later in 'The Boarding House', a separate establishment located in the same premises as the College and the school.

In these early years the number of students remained disappointingly low and with its meagre resources the College remained vulnerable. Its main strength lay in the men and women of spirit who managed and served it through these difficult years. Though they occasionally added to its problems they also assured its future – a few of them are pictured on these pages.

Augustus de Morgan.

Professors of 1849

Augustus De Morgan was a famous mathematician and one of the most distinguished Professors on the original list. He was Professor of Mathematics in University College, London, and he took no fees for his part-time lectures in the 'Ladies College'. He resigned in 1850 probably because he found the pupils so ill-prepared in his subject.

William Sterndale Bennett taught harmony and vocal music, 1849–1856. These subjects were more often taught to women and it is perhaps not surprising that he continued through seven years; maybe he found his pupils reasonably well-prepared for his classes.

William Sterndale Bennett.

EARLY DAYS AND WOMEN WITH INFLUENCE

The Lady Visitors: Women with Influence

The ladies pictured are some of the forty Lady Visitors without whom the new College would not have been sufficiently respectable for daughters of middle-class families to attend. The student, who might be as young as thirteen years, would be accompanied to the door of the College and there the Lady Visitor would take over. The group was an ever-present force within the College. The attendance of each member was organised on a roster and they sat-in as chaperones in the lectures. Their duties were defined:

*Every Visitor will endeavour to uphold decorum and silence in the Institution, and maintain in her Class Room attention and punctuality.

*With a view to the health of the Pupils, the Lady Visitors are requested to direct their attention to the ventilation and the general comfort of the rooms.

*It is hoped that the Young Ladies will look to the Lady Visitors as Friends to whom they may come for advice and assistance.

In the early years some ladies undertook these duties for the pleasure of attending lectures they wished to hear.

There were only part-time professors and originally, virtually no administrative staff. It was at first primarily a day-college with students attending only certain lectures and perhaps only once or twice a week. The Lady Visitors provided a means of communication and organisation within the College. They acted as councillors to the students and liased with members of committees. Those Ladies able to undertake the discipline of committee work might serve on the Council.

It was not easy to find enough people willing to give their time freely and with dedication to maintain this system. The number of Lady Visitors dwindled. With time and social change and also as the administration of the College was formalised their role became less important. However, forty years were to pass before these successors to the original Committee of Ladies, named above the Professors in the first Prospectus, finally disappeared and were mentioned no more in descriptions of the College.

Mrs Augustus de Morgan (Sophia Elizabeth Frend) – Member of the Original Committee of Ladies.

Lady Pollock – Member of the Original Committee of Ladies.

Mrs Hensleigh Wedgwood (Frances Mackintosh) – Member of the Original Committee of Ladies and later of Council.

Mrs Henry Busk (Mary Anne Le Breton) – Member of Council.

Lady Belcher.

Lady Charles Crompton (Caroline Fletcher).

EDUCATING WOMEN

STUDENTS, STAFF AND COUNCIL 1860s

A Resident Student

Meta Brock, later Mrs Morgan Williams, entered College as a resident student in 1861. She wrote 38 years later of her experiences there.

'My father, who held very enlightened ideas about girls education very far in advance of his time, sent his daughters up to Bedford College, to be educated.

'The fees were low. It was not intended for the daughters of rich men and I do not think any of us came from wealthy homes. We occupied two houses in Bedford Square. The lower rooms were class rooms, whilst the boarders all slept in the attic floor. We had no study bedrooms. We slept four in a room, we made our own beds, we filled our own baths, we cleared the tables after meals, we did many household tasks which nowadays are thought a waste of time for students. The College Library was our only dining and sitting room. But we were very happy. We lived under the wise and pleasant rule of Miss Thomas, who in her younger days, before her deafness unfitted her for the work, was one of the most judicious and delightful of guardians. Our studies were necessarily somewhat different from those of to-day. Of course our appliances were very inferior; we had no laboratory; no well appointed art studio; none of the many helps now thought essential to study; there were no degrees; no certificates for women.

'We worked because we loved our work, not because we hoped to put BA after our names. And for the same reason we were more free to follow our own bent in study, as the College course was not arranged with any view of preparing for Degrees. All were obliged to take five subjects, but were not permitted to take more than seven. The younger students were obliged to take Latin and Mathematics, as the College authorities set their faces resolutely against students coming to College to learn the lighter subjects only. The limit of seven subjects, too, was excellent, for, taken thoroughly, they were quite sufficient to fill up a student's time, and the arrangement went far to prevent superficial study. And that with a large experience of Intermediate and Higher Education I venture to say the education given at Bedford College in those days, in spite of inferior premises, in spite of want of modern appliances, was equal to any that is given in any educational establishment to-day. I use the word

William Russell.

education in what I consider its true sense, *viz*, the drawing out and training of the mental faculties, so as to give their owner the best possible use of them. It seems to me quite natural that it should have been so for hardly any students came to the College who were not eager to learn, and the professors in those days, Mr Richard Hutton, Mr Beesly, Dr Russell, Dr Gardiner, and others, possessed in an eminent degree the power of interesting those who were privileged to learn from them. There may be as good teachers to-day – it is impossible there can be better ones.

'Everywhere Bedford College influence has stimulated the old students to work for woman's advancement, socially and intellectually, everywhere they have given a helping hand to improve her position.'

Staff

Henrietta Busk, a day-student in 1861 recalled those who organised and administered. 'In the very early days of the College a most portly and responsible man of the name of Drover kept the door, and also all of

George Macdonald.

us students, in order, and I believe he was also feared by some of the more timid Lady Visitors.'

Jane Martineau, one of the Lady Visitors and a Reid Trustee, was the hard working Honorary Secretary of the College for 21 years from 1855. 'As far as the students were concerned the next person in importance with whom we had to do was the Lady Resident who in my day was that gracious lady Miss E S Barclay who held sway from 1854–1871. To her we paid our fees, her room adjoined and had a door into the waiting room where we collected before going up into class, and into her room the Professors used to go on arriving to fetch the attendance book of their class, before they too went to the class room.

'We had but little opportunity of conversation with our professors between the classes, though sometimes we stayed during the five minute interval to ask some questions.'

Two Professors

George Macdonald educated at Aberdeen and appointed in 1859 to teach English Language and Literature was the ninth person to hold that position showing the rapid turnover of the early staff. The subject had been popular since the masterly teaching of the Rev Alexander Scott in 1849–50. George Macdonald resigned in 1867 when teaching standards were to be checked and asked for it to take effect at once; he was opposed to scrutiny by outsiders. He later wrote a number of fanciful and idealistic novels. At the time of his Golden Wedding (1901) and also of his death (1905) many of his former students wrote in the Magazine in fulsome praise of his teaching.

William James Russell was educated at University College, London, and returned there as assistant to the Professor of Chemistry in 1857. In Bedford College, as Professor of Natural Philosophy 1860–70, he is credited with conducting the first practical science classes for women where they assisted with the experiments and, as one of them wrote, 'thereby learnt some mechanics, physics, optics, electricity and chemistry.'

Dr Russell had a distinguished career in chemistry being, from 1872, a Fellow of the Royal Society and later President of the Chemical Society and of the Institute of Chemistry. He was a member of the Council of the College from 1878 and its Chairman 1887–1903, this was a period when many important developments in College were planned and achieved.

STUDENTS, STAFF AND COUNCIL 1860s

Early Members of Council

ELISABETH REID 1789-1866 organised and funded the foundation of the College in 1849. She had long been thinking about the possibility of establishing such a 'Ladies College'. Mrs Sophia De Morgan wrote of her that 'her plans were not as practical as her intentions were good'. She was able to act on her intentions when in later life, she gained help and advice from men experienced in education and women of like mind. A student, Henrietta Busk, wrote later of Mrs Reid 'Her gently sympathetic manner and the quiet unobtrusive way in which she came among us, asking about our difficulties, encouraging us to persevere and overcome them, will always remain precious memories to those who were students in those days. Mrs Reid's desire to keep as much in the background as possible and to make all her friends think that she was doing no more than they were for the College set us all an example which we shall not easily forget'. She was a member of the Council from the beginning and intermittently until 1864.

ANNA SWANWICK 1813-1899 was an early student of the College and together with her mother was amongst the first Lady Visitors. She represented the Lady Visitors on Council 1857-61, and later, 1884-89, held the office of Visitor. She was one of the few learned women of her day. Her publications include a number of original works and many well-used translations from German and Greek dramatists. Though she attended the best girls' school in Liverpool, her later studies were at home and in Germany. She worked hard for the education of others, particularly women, and became involved with the needs of Women's Suffrage and other reforms. In 1899, she spoke at the College Jubilee Celebrations, as ex-President of the Students Association, and noted that her schooling was so meagre that she felt like the Peri excluded from Paradise, and often longed to assume the costume of boys, to attend their school, and to learn Latin, Greek and Mathematics, which were then regarded as essential to a liberal education.

ERASMUS A DARWIN 1804-1881 one of the three men who held the original funding money of the College in Trust and by virtue of that was a member of the original Council. As Chairman of Council, 1851-1869, he guided a very disparate team with perspicacity and humour through difficult times. He continued as Visitor for a further ten years, 1869-79. Erasmus was the older brother of Charles; the Darwin and Wedgwood families which were interconnected by marriage, maintained their connection with the College for many years.

WILLIAM SHAEN 1820-1887, was from a public-spirited, non-conformist family, educated at University College, London, and later much connected with that Institution and with the University of London where he served on Senate and as the Clerk of Convocation. He was a strong advocate of the admission of women to Degrees in the University of London. He was a member of the Council of Bedford College intermittently from 1850 and Chairman of Council, 1880-87. He helped in the formation of the London School of Medicine for Women and was a benefactor of Girton, Newnham and Somerville Colleges.

THESE TWO MEN were of the small group which in their service to Bedford College showed their belief that the education of women was of importance to all in society.

Other men of like-mind who served the Council in early years were Philip Le Breton, Albert Dicey, Joshua G Fitch, Richard H Hutton, Rev Mark Pattison and Nevil Story-Maskelyne.

This decorative panel was originally used in an appeal for money for the College in 1913.

9

EDUCATING WOMEN

THE REID TRUST, WOMEN WITH POWER

Eliza Bostock, Jane Martineau and Eleanor Smith were three ladies who had a great deal of power in the College in its second decade. Mrs Reid had worked with Eliza and Jane in the late 1850s providing anonymously, through them, money for scholarships and prizes for the College students; they were friends whom she could trust. In 1860 with a sum of £2000 invested to provide them with funds she established the three ladies as Managers of the Boarding House (for resident students) and enabled them, and not the College Council, to acquire the lease of the necessary second house in Bedford Square part of which they let to the College. On her death in 1866 Mrs Reid's estate completed the establishment of the Reid Trust wherein the income from £16,400, amounting to about £800 annually, was to be used for the benefit of female education and the three ladies were the Trustees. The three now also became the owners of the leases of the two College houses. The control of both the money and the premises enabled the three ladies to exert a strong and independent influence on the affairs of the College at a vital point in its development.

In the mid 1860s the College was very low in student numbers and therefore in funds. But while the College was impoverished the other two institutions also crowded in the two houses in Bedford Square – the Boarding House and the School – were solvent. The situation was complicated by the fact that the College had no charter or formally adopted constitution under which to operate and to exert its influence. The Council had been unable to agree on a proposed draft Charter. Along with the financial and constitutional problems there were rumours and accusations of low academic standards.

In 1868 the three Reid Trustees used their financial power to invervene and determine a course of action. They required an outside examination of standards of teaching and insisted that the College should apply for a Charter under which to conduct its affairs. The Council complied and ordered a report on the teaching in both School and College from James Bryce, an assistant commissioner on the Royal Commission on Middle-Class Education. Unfortunately no copy of his report seems to have survived but it may have been unfavourable, particularly to the school which was very soon closed. The Reid Trustees then went further and by acting through the Board the College Council was replaced by a temporary Committee of Management to be appointed by and to include themselves. Eminent and respected people agreed to serve on this Committee which acted swiftly and firmly. The majority of the professors were confirmed in their posts but some were replaced, classes were reorganised and teaching continued. A new constitution was framed and approved and in 1869 the College was incorporated as an Association under the Board of Trade regulations for companies not trading for profit. Under the new constitution the Council with its executive power was entirely in the hands of lay persons and the employed teachers had now a solely advisory role. The Board was replaced by a new body called 'The College' which acted through a 'General Meeting' and again the teachers were excluded. The office of Visitor was established with certain powers to appoint members of The College and to allow for the airing of grievances.

It was a traumatic time and some resented the changes. But the 'Ladies College in Bedford Square', now to be called 'Bedford College', emerged clearly set once more on the

Reid Trust Poster.

College Seal 1869
Helmeted Head of Minerva (Athene).

THE REID TRUST, WOMEN WITH POWER

Elizabeth Ann Bostock.

Jane Martineau.

Eleanor Elizabeth Smith.

path towards its original aim to provide a liberal higher education for women. Its non-sectarian character was confirmed. Though the finances remained shaky, student recruitment was eventually aided by the increase in good schools for girls particularly when the Girls Public Day School Trust was started in 1872 and by the general climate of changing opinion towards women's education. The Reid Trustees had apparently intervened to a good end.

The three ladies have been variously described as masterly, taciturn, forbidding, kindly, sympathetic. No single picture emerges. They differed in character but were united in the disciplined way in which they brought the College back on to course in 1868 and then continued to influence its affairs in subsequent years both as Reid Trustees and as Managers of the Boarding House. They remained unmarried, which is a requirement for being one of the Trustees, and continued their work with the Trust in their respective lifetimes. Each of them was involved with duties outside the College; Eleanor Smith was well-known in the intellectual circles of Oxford for her educational and suffragist interests. Over the years the Reid Trustees made grants to the College including scholarships, subsidies to Professor's departments and money spent on buildings, books and apparatus. The Trust is still in existence at the time of publication.

The Secretary of the Reid Trust
Rachel Notcutt (1841–1921) was a student in 1868 and soon afterwards a resident helping in the Boarding House in both Bedford Square and York Place, we are told of the affection and esteem in which she was held. She was assistant in the Department of Latin (1881–91), Librarian (1883–95) and Member of Council (1891–1901, 1909–13). An extract from her obituary by Margaret Tuke in the BC Magazine 1921: 'Of late Miss Notcutt has been best known in the College through her Secretaryship of the Reid Trustees – a small body of women with whom it lies to administer the fund left by Mrs Jesser Reid for the advancement of women's education. Miss Notcutt was made a trustee in 1882 in succession to Miss Martineau and acted as Secretary from the first. Through this office she was brought into contact with many students both of Bedford and other Colleges, especially those who held fellowships and scholarships offered by the Trustees. She made a point of knowing the Scholars personally; she befriended them when they were in trouble or difficulties; she cared for their health and gave to many of them a delightful holiday at Penmaen in the Gower country, a house, which Miss Bostock her friend and the early benefactor of the College, placed at her disposal in the summer months. The link thus formed with the "Reid" Scholars did not cease with the college days. She remained the councillor and friend of many throughout her life.'

Rachel Lydia Notcutt.

11

EDUCATING WOMEN

YORK PLACE, BAKER STREET 1874

The Houses

When the leases expired in Bedford Square two houses were acquired at 8 and 9 York Place which was part of the east side of Baker Street just north of Paddington Street. These were elegant houses in a good district. They were adapted to hold both the teaching rooms and the accommodation for residents. The move was made in 1874 but in to very makeshift quarters until the adaptations were finished at Easter, 1875.

The entrance led to a well-proportioned Central Hall built at the

The Central Hall.

back of the houses. It gave access to the basement laboratories, the dining room and classrooms and also, at the rear of the houses where the stables had previously stood, more classrooms, a large lecture room and a fine studio with a north light. The library and

The College in York Place, Baker St, viewed from York St.

more formal rooms were on the first floor.

Residence rooms were on the upper two storeys. This continued the same arrangement as in Bedford Square. The rooms were either shared or single, with or without a fireplace, all individually furnished but each with a washstand, jug and basin behind a screen. Housemaids brought brown cans of hot water to the rooms each day but in the bathroom on each floor there were hot water pipes and hot water for baths, a welcome change from the Bedford Square days.

By virtue of their financial control the Boarding House Managers were again able to ensure that teaching activities and day students were strictly segregated from the boarders. The professors and the day students had to put up with many petty restrictions some of which were designed to prevent them using Boarding House resources. For the

A Resident's Room.

The Library.

first dozen or so years in York Place this attitude persisted but it then waned as people and conditions changed. In the late 1880s the spirit of College life was fostered first by communal use of the Common Room and Library and then by organisation of societies and clubs.

The Art School
Drawing had been taught since 1849 reputedly attracting the younger pupils. In York Place with its studio and fine equipment, an Art School developed which had enthusiastic and clever students but numbers remained low and integration with other subjects in the curriculum was difficult.

The Art Studio.

The sketch of the studio was made in 1891 and shows a young art student. It was in 1894 that the College received its first Treasury Grant and shortly afterwards a General Meeting of the graduates and undergraduates passed a resolution which was to be communicated 'to all students who attend College with their hair down'. Basically the resolution said that as the Government recognised us to be a Women's College of full University status and as some who attended were youthful, all students should adopt during College hours a style of dress which did not allow of any confusion with secondary girls' schools which might call themselves colleges.

The Magazine
The *Bedford College Magazine* was started in 1886 and it gained a regular format in 1894 when it became the organ of the newly-founded Bedford College Students Association, BCSA, which represented both past and present students. The magazine was printed by the Women's Printing Society Ltd at Whitcomb Street, London WC with a front cover

design which remained unchanged for 25 years. There was an issue of this main magazine each term but there were also other intermittent productions. *Bedford Knowledge* of the early 1890s was a humorous magazine. Occasionally *The Owlet* appeared, a production solely for present students. The main *Bedford College Magazine* contains a glorious mixture of reports from staff, students and former students on events both official and informal, literary efforts, College announcements and births, marriages and deaths.

The Boating Club
In June, 1889, the Magazine reported the start of the Boating Club. 'About the end of the Lent Term it occurred to an enthusiastic and enterprising student that it would be a good thing for Bedford College to add a Boating Club to its numerous existing clubs and societies. The idea was very favourably received, and by the end of the term a pretty clear outline of the proposed club had been formed. A copy of the rules was issued at the beginning of the Easter term, and the Club already numbers fifteen members, and bids fair to be a great success. An agreement has been made with the owner of the boats on the ornamental water in Regent's Park, by which a boat is to be at the disposal of the club each morning between the hours of 8.45 and 10.45, when lessons in rowing and steering are given. The Club has been practising since May 13th, and all the members appear greatly pleased, especially the rowing-lessons, which are excellent. The colours of the Club are pink and grey; the costume consists of a grey skirt and cap, and a blouse of striped grey and pink tennis-flannel.'

It was a rule that 'members appear at practice in the costume of the Club'. In the 70 or more years of the Club's existence the costume changed many times. By 1892 it had changed to 'blue serge skirt, a cream or white blouse and a white sailor hat with blue band'.

The Boating Club in Regent's Park.

EDUCATING WOMEN

THE SHAEN WING
1890

In 1886 it was found that commitments to science courses requested by the students could not be fulfilled because the laboratories were inadequate. Three purpose-built laboratories were needed for physics, chemistry and biology. An appeal was made for money but the response was slow and students numbers (c 112) not sufficient to ensure high fee income. However, the decision was made to expand, the leases of three adjoining houses at the back of the premises were acquired and a new wing built there, connected by a corridor from the Central Hall. The new wing was to be a memorial to William Shaen. This was not the end of expansion on this site, subsequently, between 1896 and 1908 three additional houses in York Place were added to the premises, allowing more adaptation to the total of eight houses.

The Empress Frederick received by the Students.

Opening of The Shaen Wing

The Empress Frederick, daughter of Queen Victoria, opened the Shaen Wing in March, 1891. This was the first royal visit to the College and was fully and delightfully reported in the press with sketches of the College and its personalities. The success and development of the College in its drive towards higher education for women were both very newsworthy. After welcoming words the Empress moved through the avenue of graduates and undergraduates in their academic gowns from the Central Hall to the new wing.

The Physics and Chemistry Laboratories

The tour started at ground level with the Physics Laboratory (37ft by 35ft) which boasted a concrete floor for stability, hot water pipes for heating and excellent up-to-date equipment.

The Empress and entourage then climbed to the top floor to the Chemistry Laboratory and noted its particular ventilation and excellent laboratory benches and fittings. The Royal visitor spoke with the Chairman of Council, Dr Russell, in terms of warmth of Dr Hofmann whom her father, the late Prince Consort, had brought to England to introduce the Giessen teaching of chemistry into this country and, enquiring of Professor

The Chemistry Laboratory.

THE SHAEN WING 1890

The Physics Laboratory.

(2 days a week). There was a fourth laboratory, also in the basement and used for both Botany and Geology. The Council reported with pride after the opening of the Shaen Wing that an effort was made to provide good equipment for all four so 'that the Laboratories, fully and fitly furnished, should stand forth second to none'.

The Laboratories were described in detail in promotional pamphlets and it was noted that during the hours when the Chemistry Laboratory was open 'The professor or an assistant will always be present to superintend and help the students, and every assistance will be given to independent and research work'.

In December, 1896, two laboratories for Botany and Geology were set up in the new extension into No 10 York Place. The vacated basement laboratory was then available for Physiology and also for Bacteriology and other teaching for the new Hygiene Course.

Crompton about his class, seemed surprised that chemistry was not more studied by the ladies of the College.

The Residents' Rooms

Below the Chemistry Laboratory were two storeys of residence rooms. The Empress Frederick had come to open Shaen Wing and she would do so only after a very thorough inspection of it. An account of the visit in the College Magazine says 'After visiting the upper storey of resident students' rooms and coming down to those on the level of the lower storey, it was suggested that they were only a repetition of what she had seen. But she had the idea that those might by in a more workaday condition than those she had visited, and she immediately went through them also'. Only after all this were the waiting dignitaries in the Large Lecture Theatre joined for the gracious speeches which ended the visit.

The Other Laboratories

The Shaen Wing was built without a Biology Laboratory, probably because of representations by Eliza Bostock that biology (equated in her mind with vivisection and the views of Charles Darwin, both of which were abhorred by William Shaen) was not a suitable subject for the memorial nor for the students. The Council acknowledged these feelings by omitting Biology from the Shaen Wing but it converted the previous physics laboratory, entered via the Central Hall, for Biology, both animal (4 days a week) and vegetable

Fair Physicists.

A Resident's Room.

15

EDUCATING WOMEN

COLLEGE WOMEN OF THE 1890s

Miss Emily Penrose
Welcome changes were afoot when in 1893 Emily Penrose was appointed as the first academic and resident Principal. In 1894 the Managers of the Boarding House gave to the Council of the College both the leases of the premises and the furniture, fittings and control of the Boarding House; from that time the Principal was the Head of the whole College including the residence.

Degree examinations of the University of London were opened to women in 1878 and Bedford students had been gaining BA, BSc and Masters Degrees from the early 1880s (see page 83). Students now needed guidance in choosing which qualification to enter for. Miss Penrose, who was herself the Head of Ancient History, was able to advise all of the students about their courses and academic progress. In addition to the academic advice, she stressed to them the importance of participation in the College community. Under her skilled leadership the college became enlivened with a corporate spirit and many new activities were encouraged.

Miss Emily Penrose.

Dr Catherine Raisin in the Botany Laboratory.

Dr Catherine Raisin
The first woman to be Head of an academic department in the College was Catherine Alice Raisin. She had studied for her Degree at University College when certain classes there were opened to women in the late 1870s and in 1884 she graduated with Honours in Geology and then continued with research. She came to Bedford College as a demonstrator in botany, 1886-1890. At this time such assistant staff had no fixed scale of payment and the fees for most of them were a charge on the salary of the professor under whom they worked. In 1890 Miss Raisin succeeded Grenville A J Cole as Head of the Geology Department, a position which she held until she retired in 1920. Her outstanding teaching and administrative abilities were further evidenced by the facts that she was Head of the Botany Department 1891-1908, resident Vice-Principal of the College 1898-1901, and was responsible for the sub-department of Geography 1916-1920.

Miss Raisin attained her DSc in 1898 and in 1902 was elected a Fellow of University College. She is pictured teaching in the Botany Laboratory in No 10 York Place. The Bedford science students at the turn of the century could be taught by women who had achieved full recognition in their subjects, something which had not been available to previous generations.

Miss Henrietta Busk
Henrietta Busk (1845-1936) pictured aged 35 years, entered the College in 1861 having previously been a pupil at the school in the same building. Her parents were friends of Mrs Reid and her mother was a Lady Visitor. Henrietta finished her course in 1864. The College then became her main interest and she served it for the rest of her life. She worked at administration when there was no money to pay for officers. It was Miss Busk who compiled and paid for the first edition (1888) of the College Calendar because she thought the history of the early years might disappear for want of records. In 1889 with the Hon Secretary, Miss Lucy Russell, she prepared statements and statistics which eventually led to a Treasury Grant being made to Bedford College in 1894, the first time a Women's College received such a grant. In 1892 she founded the Students' Loan Fund for the Training Department and in 1894 the Bedford College Students Association. She masterminded the Jubilee celebrations and was active in the 1903 appeal for

COLLEGE WOMEN OF THE 1890s

extension funds.

Miss Busk assisted her brother Edward in his campaigns to have the London Degree examinations open to women and then to form a federal teaching University. Her work in general education included the Teachers Guild and the Conference of Education Associations.

In 1926–1928 she was President of the Bedford College Old Students Association. Amongst her personal benefactions were the tower clock over the quadrangle in Regent's Park, destroyed in the bombing of 1941, and the decorative entrance gates still in use in Regent's Park. When she died in 1936 at the age of ninety, the struggle for the establishment of university education for women was a thing of the past; she had been a member of the College Council since 1882 with a gap of only four years. Truly a stalwart friend of Bedford College.

The Greek Plays

The first Greek play to be presented by the students was Euripides 'Iphigenia in Tauris' given in Greek at York Place in June, 1887. Sophocles' Antigone was performed in December, 1902 and it was well reviewed by the national press. From

Miss Henrietta Busk.

The Times of December 18th: 'In one respect the production of the play was remarkable, for the cast was entirely composed of ladies, and this idea, though very unclassical, was fully justified by the excellent result.' 'That these girls should produce a Greek play so successfully should certainly be some consolation to the advocates of the old-fashioned idea of literary culture.'

The College Magazine reported 'Miss Tchaykovsky, the Conductor, had been holding Choir and Orchestra practices ever since the beginning of the term'. 'A stage was erected for the audience in the front dining-room, and, as the seats were in tiers, all could see comfortably. In the limited space afforded by the back dining-room, Orchestra, Chorus and Actors had to play their respective parts. Every inch of the room was put to the best use and the clever contrivance of stage and proscenium elicited much praise from the audience. Mr Thomson and the members of the Art School earned our warmest thanks for designing and painting of the scenery. The lighting was admirable too: electric lights framed the arch on the side away from the spectators so there was plenty of light and no discomfort.'

The Cast and Chorus of Antigone 1902.

17

EDUCATING WOMEN

STUDENT FUNDING. YORK PLACE LIBRARY

College Scholarships

Some scholarships, paid for by Mrs Reid, were offered for students in 1852 and for potential students seven years later. Other College scholarships and prizes followed. There was also a loan fund for Training Department students (1892) and though very small, it was available later to any student in special need.

In 1889, a lady wrote, enclosing a cheque for £20, 'I hope by degrees to repay the scholarships that I held at Bedford College from November, 1874, to July, 1876. As I was at that time not at all well off, the value of the first scholarship was increased, partly by Council, and partly owing to the kindness of Miss Bostock. Now, from family circumstances and some success in my profession, I am able to repay the help which was so valuable to me'.

Funding of Students

The report of Council for 1890–91 discussed a number of anxieties including the funding of students. 'It has been disappointing each term to have to record a smaller number of students as compared with the corresponding term of last session, without being able to assign any definite reason for this check to the numbers in College. It may possibly arise from the fact that other Colleges for women, by reason of State aid, private benefactions and other endowments, can offer to their students greater pecuniary advantages than can Bedford College, which is absolutely without any permanent endowment. To many students, specially those adopting teaching as a profession, the greater value of a Scholarship, and the longer length of time for which it is tenable, is not only an attraction, but of necessity a very important factor in determining their choice of College.'

The Council need not have worried. The turning point was the grant of £500 made to the College in 1894–5 by the Technical Education Board of the London County Council in exchange for free tuition for up to six scholars and a place for themselves on the College Council. As the histogram shows, this Local Authority grant for scholars heralded the very dramatic changes in funding for students that followed throughout the Twentieth Century.

NUMBER OF STUDENTS AT BEDFORD COLLEGE 1850-1984

The effects can be seen of the two world wars, the 1963 Report of the Robbins Committee and the changes in the availability of financial help for students.

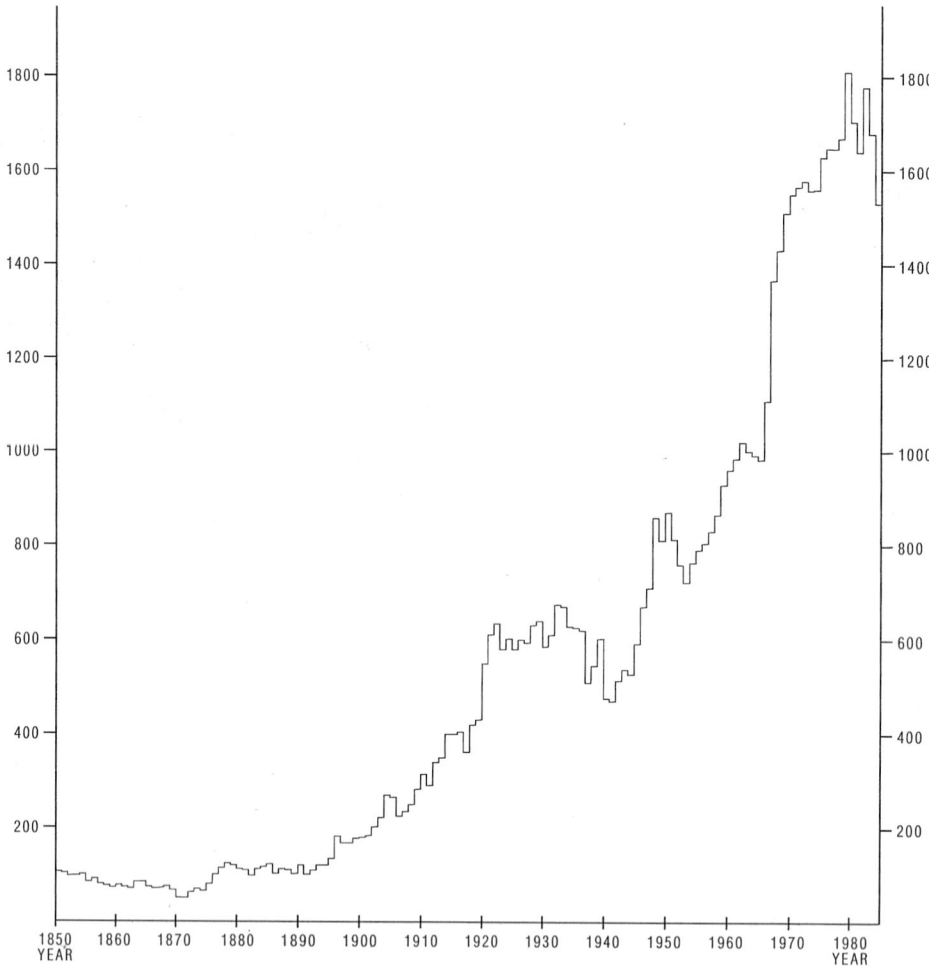

The Library.

The Library Rooms

The library and study on the first floor were heated by a fire in cold weather. The library's collection started from a donation of Mrs Reid's books and was added to by gifts, collection and purchase so that the volumes came to cover what was required even on the science side.

Some splendid and rare volumes were given to the library and it benefited also from the continual purchase of books paid for by the Reid Trust. These books were distinguished by a bookplate showing their origin. The council had to approve the design of the bookplate and the design shown was one rejected in 1894.

Miss Rachel Notcutt had been librarian since 1872 along with her other duties in the College and Residence. In 1886 a Library Committee, serviced by the librarian, organised loans and discipline. A full-time librarian was appointed in 1902.

STUDENT FUNDING. YORK PLACE LIBRARY

SOURCES OF FUNDING FOR BEDFORD COLLEGE STUDENTS 1854–1984

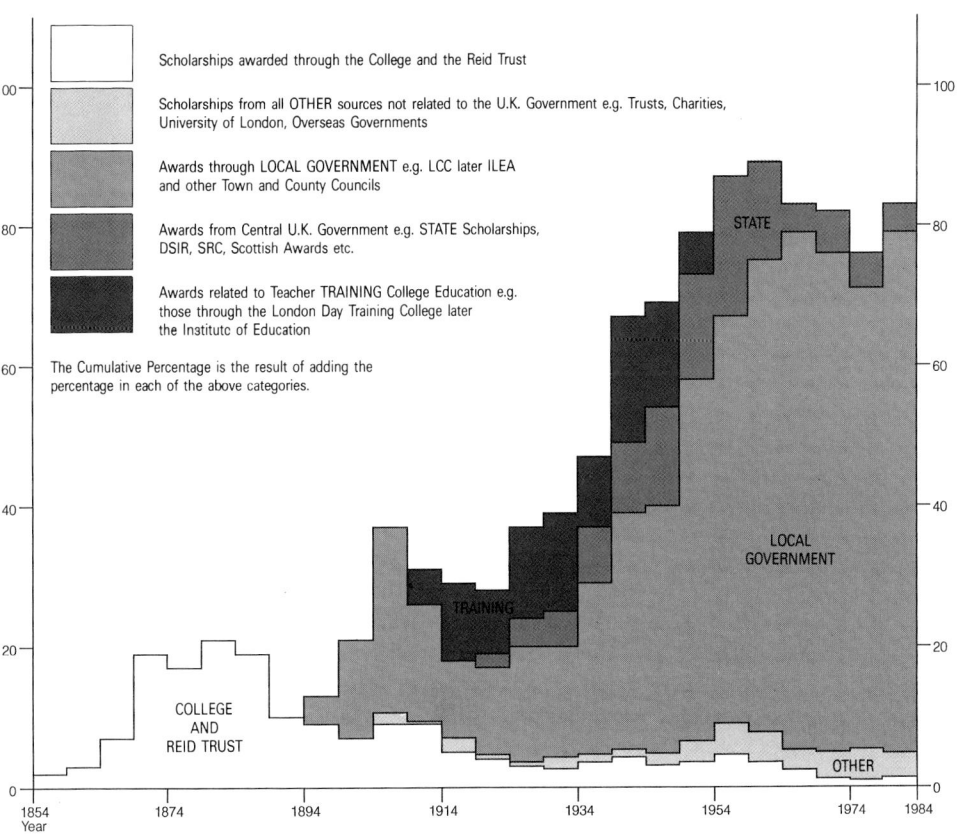

A Reid Trust Bookplate.

By 1905 the library had grown to 11,000 volumes housed in four interconnected rooms.

The library benefited from two memorials to Mrs Reid. The old students' memorial had included 300 volumes with mahogany bookcases to hold them and a terracotta plaque.

Miss Bostock had given six handsome stained glass windows in one of the library rooms fronting on to Baker Street. When the College moved to Regent's Park the books and bookcases were easily transferred. With somewhat more difficulty the windows were removed and successfully re-installed in the Wernher Reading Room of the new Library. They were destroyed in the bombing of the second world war.

The Central Library Room with Bostock-Reid Memorial Windows.

19

EDUCATING WOMEN

COMMUNITY AND SOCIAL LIFE IN YORK PLACE

Community and Social Life
From the slow start in the 1880s, social life grew rapidly in the next twenty years. Freshers were welcomed by seniors and friendships grew up around residence or shared activities in College clubs.

Societies and Clubs reported in each issue of the magazine and at the turn of the century there were plenty of clubs including the following.

Architectural	Natural Science
Boating	Old Students
Chemical	Athletic
Christian Union	Photographic
Classical	Philanthropic
Common Room	Reid Literary
Debating	Residents Library
Dramatic	Shakespeare
Fencing	Reading
Fire Practice	Sketching
Gymnasium	Stamp Collecting
Hockey	Swimming
Impromptu	Tea
Debating	Tennis
Musical	

The *Boating Club*, now ten years old, claimed to be the largest College Club with 113 members. The Regent's Park Boatman still coached the students and there were very popular annual races.

The *Hockey Club*, along with Tennis and Swimming, joined the London University Colleges Club for their matches; the London University Athletic Union formed a women's section only in 1911. The group picture taken in 1905, is the College Trial Hockey. Olive Monkhouse, third from the right in the middle row, was later Secretary of the College (1919–1948) and after the Second World War was largely responsible for the speed and success of the re-building scheme. Though hockey matches were organised between the Colleges there was also a well-supported Arts v Science match in the College.

A Hockey Group 1905.

The *Gymnasium* was fitted out by a gift of apparatus in 1897 and a semi-official club was formed. Sargeant Sullivan's twice weekly classes in English gymnastics were replaced by a weekly class in Swedish gymnastics, less exciting but quite as useful. All the students were encouraged to this physical exercise and instruction by official College notices. 'Attendance in Laboratory and Lecture Room is a heavy tax upon time and physique; and the majority of day Students make long daily journeys in train or omnibus, leaving little time for physical recreation at home.' The

The Boating Club in Regent's Park.

COMMUNITY AND SOCIAL LIFE IN YORK PLACE

The Common Room.

magazine reported 'If anyone wants half-an-hour's diversion let her take up her stand on the roof above the gymnasium, and watch the frantic efforts of the performers below. Unwieldly lower limbs, limp arms and scattered hairpins in abundance'.

The *Common Room*, which had moved and improved over the years, was available to all the students and it was organised by the Common Room Society. In December, 1899, during the Boer war, they reported 'The progress of the war is watched very closely, and to meet the growing demand for information an Evening Paper has been added to the already long list of journals. The wall has been adorned with a Transvaal map, gaily decorated with flags, which are regulated from time to time'.

There were various *Philanthropic* ventures like the Women's University Settlement. Taking practical responsibility at home the staff-student *'Fire Brigade'*, trained by the local Fire Station, divided care of the premises between them, assembled periodically in the Central Hall to practise dealing with emergencies and held fiercely energetic fire drill for everyone.

BCSA and The College Colours

At its first formal meeting Bedford College Students Association (BCSA was for both past and present students) started consideration of College Colours and by December, 1895, after many suggestions had been considered, the badges and colours were put on sale. The badge showed the head of Minerva, in a helmet, on a shield and with the letters BCSA above. 'The gold, brown and black ribbon shows off the rather sombre badge, and yet is by no means too bright for ordinary wear.' In May, 1897, the current students, who had it seems never really taken to the brown, black, gold combination, voted that the colours worn by the Hockey Club (red and black separated by a narrower white stripe) should be adopted as College Colours. The Council wrote firmly to the BCSA to tell them that these 'shall henceforth be known as "College Colours"'. Furthermore, 'that no change in the colours now determined on can be made without reference to the Council'. So red, black and a narrow stripe of white became the 'College Colours' until changed at some time before the 1920s.

Residence

Lilian Vass (Mrs Turnpenny) recalled in 1987 her arrival and experiences as a resident student in Baker Street at the start of her studies for BA English.

'The day after arrival we were interviewed by the tutors. Residence and lectures were at Baker Street – all under one roof and I didn't even have to put my hat on. That's what I call "residence".

'If you did not sign your name in the book before breakfast at 8 am someone came to find if you were all right unless a friend had reported that you were ill. Then (except on Sundays when you made your own bed) you had to leave your room to the maids. Ours, Emma, completed fifty years service, ending as Head Housemaid. We were all fond of her.

'The food was good and we were always hungry. Breakfast we served ourselves. Lunch was a scramble as the day students joined in. Many times I've stood eating macaroni cheese from the mantelpiece.'

'. . . . to dinner. Everyone was gathering in the big Common Room. All the staff and seniors took in someone junior, at the end juniors made up a table of their own. There was also a table known as "the slum" at which you had to sit if you weren't dressed. Dinner was a formal, four course meal served by maids. Coffee was served in the Common Room.'

A Resident's Room.

21

EDUCATING WOMEN

50 YEARS OF ACADEMIC PROGRESS

The high academic standards of the College were now clear. It was firmly established as a University College. It had the best list of women students who had graduated with London Degrees. Faculties of ARTS and SCIENCE were emerging within the College which was preparing to be part of the new teaching University of London. There was still the College Associateship given as a result of a general College education but fewer were taking this as the students and their families came to value University Degrees.

Other types of training were still offered. The ART STUDIO did not take students to a professional qualification but two other departments did so. The HYGIENE DEPARTMENT trained students for professional and College Diplomas in Public Health with which they emerged to undertake social and philanthropic work and become Sanitary and Factory Inspectors or Health Visitors. These courses which trained women scientifically were praised as models for elsewhere. The TEACHER TRAINING DEPARTMENT provided many postgraduates with their teaching qualifications.

Scholarships had been donated and established for needy students. There was an excellent, catalogued Library and also a College Museum with anthropoligical, biological and geological specimens. The control of the College was in the hands of an executive Council on which women served equally with men and the academic Principal was responsible for all students. There were now more sister Institutions with which the College could compare (Girton and Newnham 1869, Somerville and Lady Margaret Hall 1879, Royal Holloway 1886).

The finances had always been on a knife edge with little or no endowment but were now assisted by grants from government and local authorities. After 50 years of relying on hard-working voluntary officers the first paid Secretary to the College had been appointed in 1898. The premises in Baker Street comprised 12 lecture rooms, 7 laboratories, 4 library rooms, the Art Studio, offices, a small gymnasium, 3 adjacent dining rooms, 2 common rooms and residence for 40 students. The total number of students was between 180 and 240 and the minimum age of entry was 16, soon to rise to 17, years.

A student's-eye-view of the academic work can be seen in the College Letters which appeared each term in the College Magazine. Full reports were given there also on many serious extra-curricular events. These included an Inaugural Lecture each session given by an eminent guest speaker, occasional lectures, library acquisitions, earnest inter-collegiate debates, papers read by students to their subject Societies and Saturday morning classes organised for working science teachers.

Sketches at Bedford College for Women: from The Daily Graphic.

50 YEARS OF ACADEMIC PROGRESS

COLLEGE LETTERS

Arts

The extra half-hours for BA Greek seem to meet with general approval; but the after four o'clock lectures seem unusually numerous; indeed, some unfortunates have only one evening a week free, which causes much tearing of hair to the presidents of various societies. Dec 1897

One word more. Does the female mind, however highly educated, always 'dote on the milingtary', or why, when the sound of a band and a marching regiment came down Baker Street, did every student in the Library fly to the windows (and even the balcony) 'to see the pretty soldiers go by'? Dec 1897

Science

The new room for Physical research is now quite finished and in use for work on the variation of specific heat with temperature. New platinum resistance thermometers have been obtained for this work and are now being standardised. March 1898

A certain amount of excitement was caused one afternoon by the fact that one student was suddenly seen to be in flames. However, she lay down quite calmly, and was immediately knelt upon by her nearest neighbours, so that all danger was over before most people knew what had happened and they only caught a glimpse of her as she lay 'smiling and smouldering' on the floor. We consider the behaviour of those concerned a credit to the College and to the cause of women's education. June 1898

The lecture given by Sir Oliver Lodge on 'Electricity and Matter' was much enjoyed by Science students, and great have been the discussions which have followed it. March 1903

The Bodichon Art Studio: named in 1895 for Madame Bodichon, Barbara Leigh-Smith, friend, benefactress and former Art student.

Hygiene Department

We are becoming hardened to the contemplation of the ubiquitous microbe in his thousands in drinking water – especially that consumed in East London – though some of us are shocked by the revelation of the conditions which in the common or garden filter enable him to increase and multiply. March 1899

Bacteriology has been our *piece de resistance*. July 1899

A delightful trip on the Sewage Department's steamer down the river to Barking; another to the West London Water Works; .... in one week both Welford's Dairy and the Farrington Street Meat Market .... seeing the making of sausages by 6.30 am .... the seizing by HM's meat inspector of a consignment of cats sent from Holland as rabbits .... We have learnt to take samples of food for analysis, and .... the methods to be pursued in registering bakehouses. March 1903

Training Department

The work this term is mostly happily varied by the opportunities that are afforded us of visiting schools, and by 'outside' lectures. It is a pleasure to hear the lesson of a good teacher in the full swing of work, now that we have had a little experience – always supposing that we forget for the moment to criticise. The discipline which allows an amount of freedom, that in our novice hands would pass into rowdiness, fills us with awe and wonder, tempered with delight. June 1898

Studio

We have been most unlucky in our models this term .... fallen ill or basely deserted us .... our model is a charming old lady, whom we are all drawing or painting with unabated energy. March 1903

We go down to Kew with camp-stools and painting boxes .... settle on the tow path. June 1903

Intercollegiate Teaching

In 1902 the staff expressed concern that the College was not able to accommodate intercollegiate classes because they were attended by both men and women. Our students went elsewhere but we could not reciprocate.

Council and a Special General Meeting responded and recognised formally that in any future accommodation, men might attend the lectures with women – a far cry from the need for chaperones. Although there was then a financial deficit each year, and though a move to a new site was contemplated, immediate action was decided upon. With the help of donations they leased an adjacent house, No 7, York Place, made communicating doors and converted the ground-floor room to accommodate men and women for some of the Honours lectures. Fully reciprocal intercollegiate teaching was now underway.

'We came to York Place by Horse Bus' 1899.

EDUCATING WOMEN

JUBILEE CELEBRATIONS 1899

In its Jubilee year, 1899, the College planned grand celebrations. Events covered three days, 22nd to 24th June; the Bedford College Students Association had a Conference, the Council had a Public Meeting and a Conversazione and on the final day everyone had a Garden Party. 14,000 invitations were sent out and 60 student stewards, each distinguished by a red bow, managed the various events whilst others wore a ribbon in the College Colours or the BCSA badge.

The Conference was held in the Portman Rooms near College because although there was a large lecture room in York Place it was not adequate for the 2,503 who attended. Ten distinguished former students gave reminiscences of the last fifty years, of the teaching and of what the College had meant in their lives. At the conclusion the company crossed over to College for tea. 'The College was very prettily decorated, chiefly with large daisies and grasses, evidently brought from the fields. These harmonised beautifully with the red brick in the Central Hall. Tea was served in the Dining Hall and the South Lecture Room. Unfortunately the afternoon was so wet that the large Lecture Room had to be turned in to a cloak and umbrella room.'

The Public Meeting was more formal and held in the Theatre and Reception Rooms of the University of London in Burlington Gardens. Universities and Colleges which then admitted women all sent representatives and the event was treated as a Jubilee of Women's University Life.

At the Conversazione the College put itself on show to about 500 guests. The Chairman of Council, Dr W Russell and the Principal, Miss E Hurlbatt, received them in the vestibule leading to the study and libraries in No 8 York Place. There was tea and coffee in the Training Department, refreshments in the three lecture rooms and a String Band played in the Central Hall. There was a display of Art but the greatest interest, inevitable in a women's College in 1899, centred around the exhibition of scientific experiments in the laboratories and we take our report of these from the College Magazine.

The Large Lecture Room.

Laboratory Exhibitions
'The Science side of the College felt that great things were demanded of it, and rose to the occasion with an alacrity that astonished even itself. Never before have the laboratories been such scenes of beauty as on the night of the conversazione. Starting from the hall, a visitor of an enquiring turn of mind was conducted to the Physics laboratory, where electrical, sound, and other experiments were in full swing. Here were to be seen Röntgen ray photography, and the apparatus for wireless telegraphy, possessing a

The Dining Room.

JUBILEE CELEBRATIONS 1899

The Central Hall.

current "strong enough to kill a man". Also on view were the electrical oscillations of Hertz, and numerous other physical experiments and apparatus, modern and historical.

'Next, up the staircase illuminated with Chinese lanterns, to the Chemistry laboratory, glorious with electric light newly laid on. There were standard lamps near the different exhibits in various elegant forms; but most beautiful of all were the decorations of the sinks, which for the time being had been turned into veritable fairy pools. Wonderfully delicate jets of water were made into fountains, illuminated with suspended electric lights and falling into pools of water filled with greenery, rushes, and yellow irises.

'The most fascinating feature in this laboratory – next to the fountains – was a chemical clock, registering Greenwich time, according to the notice, but in reality a trifle slow. This little defect may be ascribed to an excess of hospitality, because, as was explained, "we do not want to hurry our visitors away". Other interesting exhibits in Crystallography, Metallurgy, and dye-stuffs were to be seen also.

'Downstairs again to the Zoology and the Physiology laboratories. In the former were all the quaint "beasties" enumerated on the programme.

'In the Physiology laboratory the microbe and bacilli slides divided the honours with elaborate physiological apparatus illustrating animal electricity.

Optical experiments were carried on in addition, and optical instruments of various kinds were on show.

'Passing next to the Botany and the Geology laboratories, one found a crowd of people grouped round the microscopes and trays of mineral exhibits artistically displayed in the two rooms.

'During almost the whole evening all six rooms were thronged with visitors, many of whom were loud in their praise of the various exhibits and of the laboratories themselves.'

The Garden Party

The College had no grounds of its own and so the Garden Party was held in the Gardens of the Royal Botanic Society which were at that time within the Inner Circle of Regent's Park. About 600 students and past students and 1,900 guests enjoyed tea, the gardens and the music of the 1st Life Guards Band.

The International Congress of Women Workers was meeting in England at that time and some guests came over from that Congress. A very large circle of students and professors, both past and present, joined hands to sing 'Auld Lang Syne'. The garden party made a most enthusiastic and brilliant termination to a very successful three days' celebration of the Jubilee of the College.

The Basement Zoology Laboratory approached by a spiral stair from the Central Hall.

Bedford College

(UNIVERSITY

TIME TABLES, 1849-1899.
(The first class is the lowest in each subject).

1849—1850 (FIRST SESSION.)

Hours.	MONDAY.	TUESDAY.	WEDNESDAY.	THURSDAY.	FRIDAY.	SATURDAY.
9.20	Bible.		Drawing.	Elocution.	Italian.	Ancient History.
10.30	Natural Science.	Ancient History.	Moral Philosophy.	Natural Science.	English Literature.	Drawing.
11.40	German.	English Literature.	Mathematics.	German.	Mathematics.	Latin.
1.10	Italian.	Astronomy and Physical Geography.	Modern History.	French.	Astronomy and Physical Geography.	French.
2.20	Vocal Music.	Harmony.	Latin.	Vocal Music.	Modern History.	

1849-50. 193 Students entered the College taking, for the most part, single classes

1879-1880 (THIRTY-FIRST SESSION.)

Hours.	MONDAY	TUESDAY.	WEDNESDAY.	THURSDAY.	FRIDAY.	SATURDAY.
10.0	English Language. Italian. 2nd Greek.	1st Latin. 3rd French.	Drawing. English History. Preparatory Eng. History. Physics, Ex. Class.	English Language. Italian. 2nd Greek.	1st Latin. 3rd French.	Drawing. English History. Preparatory Eng. History.
11.10	English Literature. 1st German. 1st Greek. Preparatory Latin.	3rd Latin. 2nd French. 4th Mathematics.	Drawing. Continental History. Senr. Physics Class.	English Literature. 1st German. Preparatory Latin.	3rd Latin. 2nd French. 4th Mathematics.	Drawing. Continental History. Senr. Physics Class.
12.25	Drawing. 3rd German. Botany.	2nd Latin. 1st French. 3rd Mathematics.	Drawing. Physics.	Drawing. 3rd German. Botany.	2nd Latin. 1st French. 3rd Mathematics.	Drawing. Physics.
1.45	Harmony. Drawing. 2nd German. Physics Ex. Class.	4th Latin. 1st Mathematics. 1st Arithmetic.	Chemistry Practice. 1st Latin Preparation.	Harmony. Drawing. 2nd German.	4th Latin. 1st Mathematics. 1st Arithmetic.	Chemistry Lectures. Perspective Drawing.
2.50	1st Vocal Music. 2nd Vocal Music.	2nd Mathematics. 2nd Arithmetic.	Biology Practice. Preparatory Eng Language. Chemistry Practice.	1st Vocal Music. 2nd Vocal Music.	2nd Mathematics. 2nd Arithmetic.	Biology Lectures. Preparatory Eng. Language.

1879-80. University of London Examinations first open to Women. 127 students in attendance. 13 students entered for University Courses.

1898-1899 (FIFTIETH SESSION.)

Hours.	MONDAY.	TUESDAY.	WEDNESDAY.	THURSDAY.	FRIDAY.	SATURDAY.
	Astronomy.	3rd Botany. 4th Greek.	2nd Botany Practice.	Astronomy. 3rd & 4th Botany Practice. 2nd Mathematics. 9.30 Chemistry Practice. (Hygiene and Prel. Sc.)		
10.0	2nd Chemistry. 3rd English 2nd Mathematics. 3rd Mathematics (A.) 3rd Physics. Physiology (B.Sc.)	1st Botany. 4th Chemistry. 5th English (B.) 3rd German. 4th Greek. 3rd Mathematics (C.)	Bacteriology. 2nd Botany Practice. 1st Chemistry (B.) 1st German. 1st Mathematics. 2nd Zoology.	3rd & 4th Botany Practice. Chemistry Practice. (Hygiene and Prel. Sc.) 3rd English. 2nd Mathematics. 3rd Mathematics (A.) 3rd Physics.	Arithmetic. 1st Botany. 5th English (B.) 3rd Mathematics (C.) Physiology B.Sc.	1st Chemistry (B.) 2nd Zoology.
11.5	2nd Botany. 5th English (A.) 1st History of Roman Literature 2nd Latin (B.) 5th Mathematics. 1st Physics (A.) (for June) Physiology (B.Sc.)	Hygiene. 4th Botany. 1st Chemistry (A.) 3rd German. 2nd Greek. 4th Mathematics. Mental and Moral Science. 1st Zoology.	Bacteriology. 4th Botany. 2nd Chemistry. 2nd French. 1st German. 2nd Latin (B.) 1st Physics (A.) (for January.) 2nd Zoology.	Chemistry Practice. (Hygiene and Prel. Sc.) 5th English (A.) 1st Geology. 2nd Greek. 2nd Latin (B.) 5th Mathematics. 1st Applied Mathematics	2nd Geology. 2nd Greek. Hygiene. 4th Mathematics. Mental and Moral Science. 1st Physics (B.) 1st Zoology.	11.0 { 2nd Chemistry. 2nd Latin (A. 3rd Physics. 2nd Zoology.
12.30	1st and 2nd English. 12.5 4th Greek. 4th Mathematics (B.) Mental and Moral Science. 12.5 Physiology (B.Sc.) 2nd Physics. Trigonometry (Elementary)	1st Chemistry (A.) Practice. 12.15 { 2nd Geology. 2nd History of Roman Literature. Latin (M.A.) Logic. 3rd Mathematics (B.) 2nd Zoology.	2nd Botany. 2nd English (Hamlet.) 3rd French (Composition.) 1st Physics (A.) (for June.)	12.5 3rd Chemistry 1st and 2nd English. 12.5. 4th Greek Trigonometry (Elementary) 2nd Physics.	12.5 1st Geology. Bacteriology. Latin (M.A.) Logic. 3rd Mathematics (B.) 1st Physics (B.)	12.5 2nd Physics Exercise. 2nd Zoology.
1.55	3rd Chemistry. Chemistry Practice. Roman History. 1st Latin. 3rd Latin. 2nd & 3rd Physics Practice.	Chemistry Pract. (Hygiene.) 1st Chemistry (A.) Pract. 4th History. 4th Latin. 6th Mathematics. Palæontology. 1st Zoology Practice.	1st Applied Mathematics. Systematic Botany. Chemistry Practice. 1st French. 2nd History. Physiology (Hygiene.)	Chemistry Practice. Greek History. 1st Latin. 5th Mathematics (B.) 2nd & 3rd Physics Practice. Physiology (B.Sc.)	Chemistry Practice 4th History. 4th Latin. 2nd Applied Mathematics 1st Physics Practice. 1st Zoology Practice.	
3.0	Chemistry Practice. 4th English (B.) 3rd Greek. Latin (B.A. Honours.) 6th Mathematics. 1st Physics (A.) (January.) 2nd & 3rd Physics Practice. Physics Practice (Hygiene.)	Chemistry Practice. (Hygiene.) Geology Practice. 4th Latin. 5th Mathematics. 1st History. 1st Zoology Practice.	Systematic Botany. Chemistry Practice. 4th English (A.) 1st French. 2nd German. 3rd History. 1st Mathematics. Physiology (Hygiene.)	Chemistry Practice. 2nd French (Lit.) 3rd Greek. 1st History. 6th Mathematics. 2nd & 3rd Physics Practice Physics Practice (Hygiene.) Physiology (B.Sc.)	Chemistry Practice. 4th English (A.) 1st Greek. 5th Latin. 6th Mathematics. 1st Physics Practice. 1st Zoology Practice.	
4.0	4.20 3rd Greek. Hygiene Physics. Latin Prose 5.0 Human Osteology.	Chemistry (Hygiene.)	4.10. 4th English (B.) 4th French (Phil.) Physiology (Hygiene.)	4.10 4th French (Lit.) Hygiene Physics. Physiology (B Sc.)		

1898-1899. 177 Students in attendance. Jubilee Year. 120 Students entered for University Courses.

26

… **for Women.**

(… **LONDON,**)

1849.

TIME TABLES, 1903-4 (FIFTY-FIFTH SESSION).

FACULTIES OF ARTS AND SCIENCE.

	MONDAY.	TUESDAY.	WEDNESDAY.	THURSDAY.	FRIDAY.	SATURDAY.	
		Greek iv. B. (c.) **Chemistry i. Practice.**	Mathematics iii. (Duplicate)	German i. for Science Students.	Mathematics iii. (Duplicate.) German ii. for Science Students.		1903-4 Current Session 270 Students in attendance 171 Students entered for University Courses In addition to Honours and Post-Graduate Courses arranged by the College, Students attend University and Inter-Collegiate lectures which do not appear in this Time Table The six Laboratories are open for purposes of Research Residence accommodation provided within the College.
	English iii. (A.) Greek iv. B. (a). Latin i. (A.) Mathematics iii (A.) **Botany ii** **Physics i** **Physics iii Practice.** **Physiology (B.Sc.)**	English iv. Lit. French ii. (A.) Greek iv. B. (a.) Mathematics v. (A.) **Botany i.** **Chemistry i. Practice.** **Chemistry ii.** Zoology ii.	Greek i. (B.) French iii. (B.) German ii. **Botany ii** **Physics i. Practice.**	English iv. (Lit.) German iii. (Lit.) Latin i. (A.) Mathematics iii **Botany ii** **Physics iii** **Physiology (B.Sc.)**	English iii. (C.) German ii Mathematics v. (A.) **Botany i.** **Chemistry ii.** **Physics i.** Zoology ii.		
5	Greek ii. Mathematics ii. Political Economy. **Botany ii. Practice.** **Physics iii. Practice.** **Physiology, Practice.**	Greek ii. Latin iv. A. (a.) Mental and Moral Science. Mathematics iv. (A.) **Chemistry i.** **Chemistry iii. Practice.** **Palæontology.** Zoology ii. Practice.	English iii. (B.) English iv (M.E.) English (C.H.L.) French iii. German iii. Latin iv. A. (b.) Political Economy. **Botany iii. Practice.** **Chemistry (Hygiene)** **Physics i. Practice.**	Latin iii. (Ext. B.A.) English iv. Conference. German iii. Hist. of Lang. Greek ii. Mathematics i. **Botany ii. Practice.** **Physics iii. Practice.** **Physiology Practice.**	Greek iv. A. (a.) Latin iv. B. (a.) Mental and Moral Science. Mathematics ii Mathematics iv. (A.) **Chemistry ii Practice** Zoology ii Practice		
	12. English iv. 12.5. English ii (A.) Greek iv. A. (a.) Mathematics iv. (B.) **Applied Mathematics i.** **Botany ii Practice** **Chemistry i.** **Physics iii. Practice.** **Phsiology Practice.**	12.5 French i. French Philology (Inter-Coll.) Greek iii. 12.30 Logic Mathematics iii. (B) **Botany iii.** **Chemistry ii. Practice.** Zoology ii. Practice.	Germanic Philology. 12.5 English i. French iii. Greek iv. B. (a) Latin ii. (B.) Latin iv. B. (a.) **Applied Mathematics.** **Botany iii. Practice.**	12 English iv. Lit. 12 30 English ii. (B.) Greek iv. B. (a) Mathematics v. (B.) **Botany ii. Practice.** **Physics iii. Practice.** **Physiology Practice.**	1.0. Germanic Philology. 12.5 English i. Latin iv. A. (a.) 12 30 Logic. Mathematics iii. (B.) **Applied Mathematics ii.** **Chemistry ii. Practice.** Zoology ii. Practice.		
	Latin i. B. Roman History. Italian. Mathematics vi. (B.) Scandinavian Philology. **Applied Mathematics ii.** **Botany iii.** **Chemistry iii. Practice.** **Physics ii** Zoology ii	French iii. (C.) History (Ext. B.A.) Mathematics i. **Chemistry iii** **Geology.** Zoology i.	French i. German Conversation. History iii. (European.) Latin ii. **Applied Mathematics i.** **Chemistry iv.** **Geology.** **Physiology.**	French History C.H.L. Greek History. Italian. Latin i. (B.) Mathematics vi. (A.) **Chemistry iii. Practice.** **Physics ii.** **Physiology (B.Sc.)**	History iii. (Constit.) Latin ii. **Applied Mathematics i.** **Chemistry iii.** Zoology i.		
	French Hons. Lit. German Hons. (Seminar.) Greek iii. Mathematics ii. Ex. Mathematics iv. (A.) **Anthropology.** **Botany iii. Practice.** **Chemistry iii. Practice.** **Physics ii. Practice.**	French ii. (C.) German Literature. German Hons. (c.) History ii. **Elocution.** **Chemistry iii. Practice.** **Geology Practice.** Zoology ii. Practice.	English Literature. German Hons. (Seminar.) Greek i. (A.) Latin iii. **Chemistry iii. Practice.** **Geology Practice.** **Mathematics iii. B. (Dupl.)** **Physics iii.** **Physiology.**	French Hons. Lit. Greek iii History ii. Mathematics vi. (B.) **Chemistry iii. Practice.** **Physics ii Practice.**	English Literature. Greek i. (A) Latin iii **Chemistry iii. Practice.** **Mathematics iii. B. (Dupl.)** Zoology i. Practice.		
	5.0 German Hons. (b.) **Botany iii. Practice.** **Chemistry iii. Practice.** **Physics iii. Practice.**	4.30 The French Romantic Drama. 4.30 German Hons. (b.) 5.30 German Hons. (a.) **Chemistry iii. Practice.** **Geology Practice.** Zoology i. Practice.	German Hons. (b.) **Chemistry iii. Practice.** **Geology Practice** **Physics ii Exercise.** **Physiology.**	Renaissance Platonism. History Ext. B.A. (Foreign.) 5.0. General Psychology. 4.30. German Hons. (b.) 5.30. German Hons. (a.) **Chemistry iii. Practice** **Physics ii Practice.**	4.30 German v. (Hist. of Lang.) 5.0. German Hons. (c.) **Chemistry iii. Practice** Zoology i. Practice.		

TRAINING DEPARTMENT FOR SECONDARY TEACHERS.

	MONDAY.	TUESDAY.	WEDNESDAY.	THURSDAY.	FRIDAY.	SATURDAY.	
	Theory of Education (M.) School Visiting (L.) Education at home & abroad (E.)	History of Education (M. & L.) Advanced Theory (E.)	School Practice (M.L. & E.)	Discussion of Essays (M.) Drill (L.)	School Practice (M.L. & E.)	Hygiene (L. & E.)	Department founded 1892, for Students holding degrees in Arts and Science. One Course, Jan.-Dec 5 Students entered 1899 16 Students entered 1903 Second Course established, Oct-June 35 Students entered M Michaelmas term L. Lent ,, E. Easter ,,
	School Visiting (L.) Ethics (E.)	Course on Curriculum (L.)	Ditto.	School Practice (M.L. & E.)	Ditto.		
	Theory of Education (M.) School Visiting (L.)	Theory of Education as to Special Subjects. Study of Special Books (E.)	Ditto.	12.30. Psychology (M.) ,, Logic (L.) ,, Discussion of Essays (E).	Course on the teaching of Arithmetic (M.) Discussion of Essays (L.)		
	School Practice (M.L. & E.)	Voice Production (M.) Psychology (L. & E.)	Ditto.	Criticism Lessons (M. & L.)	School Practice (M.L. & E.)		
	School Practice (M.L. & E.)		Ditto.	Criticism Lessons (M. & L.) Educational Problems (E.)	School Practice (M.L. & E.)		
	Course on the teaching of Geography (L.)	University Lecture on Education (M.L. & E.)			University Lecture on Education (M.L. & E.)		

HYGIENE DEPARTMENT.

	MONDAY.	TUESDAY.	WEDNESDAY.	THURSDAY.	FRIDAY.	SATURDAY.	
	Hygiene Elementary Physics	9.0 Elem. Chemistry 10.0 Elem. Chemistry Practice.	Elementary Physics Practice.	Chemistry.	Physics. Elementary Physics.		Department founded 1895 One Year's Course affords preparation for Inspectors. (a) Sanitary, Factory, Poor-Law, etc (b) Teachers of Hygiene in Schools, Training Colleges, Adult Schools, etc. c) Philanthropic workers, members of Public Administrative Bodies A Special Course is arranged for Teachers on Saturday mornings Typical appointments obtained by Students (i) H M Inspector of Factories, (ii) Sanitary Inspector, (iii) Assistant Bacteriologist to Royal Commission on Sewage Disposal (iv) Lecturer, West Riding Co Co., (v) Rent Collector under Ecclesiastical Commissioners
		Elementary Chemistry Practice.	Elementary Physics Practice.	Chemistry Practice.	Physics Practice.	11.5. Teachers' Class.	
	Elementary Chemistry.		Hygiene.	Chemistry Practice.	Physics Practice.		
			Physiology.	Bacteriology.			
			Physiology.	Bacteriology.			
			Physiology.	Bacteriology.			

Extensive and regular arrangements are made for Inspections and Practical Demonstrations.

ART SCHOOL.

	MONDAY.	TUESDAY.	WEDNESDAY.	THURSDAY.	FRIDAY.	SATURDAY.	
	Elementary Drawing Drawing from the Antique Drawing & Painting from the Draped Model.*		Elementary Drawing Drawing from the Antique Drawing & Painting from the Draped Model.*	Drawing & Painting from the Figure Model.	Elementary Drawing Drawing from the Antique Drawing & Painting from the Draped Model.*		

*Should Students desire, the model will continue sitting till 4 o'clock
Students may, subject to revision of their work by the teacher, work in the Studio at any time when no regular classes are being held
A Class for Landscape Sketching is formed in the Easter Term

EDUCATING WOMEN

A CHARTER AND AN APPEAL 1903-1909

The Charter

Discussion started in 1901 about the inadequacy of the constitution particularly because there was no representation for employed teachers of the College on the Council or Board. Change was effected when a Royal Charter was issued in January, 1909. Bedford College, as incorporated under the Board of Trade, was wound up and everything transferred to the new chartered body BEDFORD COLLEGE FOR WOMEN.

In the new body, the old College Board, or Members of the College in General Meeting, became the Governors. The new Council admitted direct representation of public bodies like the London County Council and of the Teaching Staff of the College. An Academic Board was instituted to consider and report to Council on all academic matters. It was believed that future changes in the constitution would be easier now that the College had a charter and over the years such changes were indeed made. However, the main bodies instituted in 1909 - the Governors, Council and Academic Board - were still recognisable in the constitution of the College 75 years later. The charter was revoked on 1st August, 1985 when Bedford College was 'dissolved and ceased to exist'.

The Angel Gabriel in the Central Hall

In 1901 the College received

Reposeful, Academic Baker Street.

from Mrs Morton Summer a bequest of £4,000 plus geological specimens, furniture, books and works of art including a terracotta figure of the Angel Gabriel attributed then to Luca della Robbia. The Central Hall was reorganised and the Angel Gabriel placed on a pillar beside the arches.

The Appeal

In 1903 the College decided to make an appeal for funds. There were then over 270 students and the limit for York Place was at about 250. As well as the overcrowding, the intolerable street noises and the inconvenience of adapted buildings, the lease of one house expired in 1909 and the rest in 1928. There was a deficit on the working account of each year. The appeal was to be for £150,000 for site, buildings and endowment for the future.

Work started on committees within the College raising awareness, looking for a site and seeking promises of funds. At a Garden Party in 1904 in the Botanic Gardens, Regent's Park, the Rt Hon A H D Acland, Chairman of Council, put questions and facts before past students. 'Before dealing with the questions of the Appeal, and of starting on a new site with renewed vigour, the first thing that strikes an outsider, the first question that arises is: "Is it desirable to carry on a Women's College as part of the University of London?"' .... 'Unless we can appeal to the public, get funds, the College must come to an end .... If in five or six years we cannot get the public to recognise our work, we must close. We feel we cannot go back now; if we wish to secure this recognition, we must go forward, even if we spend out of our capital. Our policy is to go forward, and five or six years will decide whether we are to live or die.'

In 1905 they went public and the press added supportive articles to the appeal letters. Influential and titled

A Scene in Electra 1909.

A CHARTER AND AN APPEAL 1903-1909

The Angel Gabriel in the Central Hall.

people associated with the College Council and the University helped to put the Appeal forward. Brochures and letters were written and distributed and formal dinners and balls were held at which subscriptions were obtained.

The Greek Play

With the experience built up from four successful productions of Greek plays the students, staff and friends combined to present a Greek play in aid of the Appeal Fund. In July, 1909, at the Royal Court Theatre they gave a performance of Sophocles' Electra in Greek. This was a great success; music had been specially composed for the occasion and was performed by some of the Queen's Hall Orchestra behind the scenes. A translation had been provided and it was reported that 'a large audience, which sat enthralled for two hours without a break, gave all the performers a great ovation at the close'. The play was repeated in December so it must also have been a financial success. An attempt was made to repeat the financial success with three performances of the Trachiniae in July 1911 at the Royal Court Theatre. The press again gave favourable comment but as the Council reported 'perhaps owing to the fact that it is one of the least known of Sophocles' plays, perhaps to the numerous other attractions of a Coronation summer, the audiences were not sufficiently large to make the production a profitable one'.

The Principal, Art Professor and Science Staff 1903.
Top row left to right: Henry Marrett Tims (Zoology Head); John Edkins (Physiology Head); Alice Lee (Physics and Mathematics Assistant); George Thomson (Art Head); Catherine Raisin (Geology and Botany Head, Vice-Principal).

Bottom row left to right: Percy Harding (Mathematics Head); Ethel Hurlbatt (Principal); Barbara Tchaykovsky (Chemistry Lecturer); Frederick Womack (Physics Head); Holland Crompton (Chemistry Head).

EDUCATING WOMEN

GRADUATION AND A NEW SITE 1909-1911

Graduation Presentation Day Events and Commemoration Celebrations

In the early 1890s when students were presented for their Degrees at Burlington House, Presentation Day was marked also by a reception held at York Place with refreshments, exhibitions and music in all of the well-decorated rooms. It was decided to use the event to make the work of the College better known to all of its ex-students and also to Heads of Girls Schools, both public and private. This was the first time that the former students had been invited individually to the College because up to 1888, when the first edition of the College Calendar was prepared, no complete list of the past students had been kept. Additionally, it took 6 weeks of hard labour by the voluntary officers to prepare address lists of the schools. No such lists then existed, they were unique and were later lent to the government 'Education Department'. 3,000 invitations were issued in 1892 and in 1893, 400–500 guests were present. In 1897 this event was re-named as Commemoration Day, it had become a pleasant and popular annual gathering for the College.

Voluntary help continued for some years, Henrietta Busk remarked 'I remember over and over again spending whole days and weeks at the College helping to address and send out invitations to the parties which were held on the University Presentation Day'. Such an event, celebrating the academic successes of that year, continued through the years though it changed its form and became separated once again from the idea of Commemoration and from the need for publicity.

Presentation Day for the graduates of 1910 was held in May, 1911, and we read in the Magazine of the events in College after the ceremony. The Principal was 'at home' at South Villa to give everyone a chance to see the future home of the College. The Dinner was the largest on record, the guests numbering 129. 'The speeches over, we made our way to Central Hall, to end the day by singing the College Songs. The roof rang with the echoes of the Boating Song and the Social Song, and the Vive-là was sung with great effect by Miss Gassett. We finished with the clasping of hands and the singing of "Auld Lang Syne" – wished one another good-night and good-bye, and many of us retired to bed, with the strains of the Graduates' Song ringing in our ears, to dream of our own Presentations in the days to come.'

Winifred Leyshon gave us the pictures of graduates, she was in later life Head of Physics at the London School of Medicine. The Vive-là, or Graduates Song, that year, mentioning every graduate by name, included the following verses.

On very thin ice
  Miss Leyshon's no skater,
The examiners found her
  'Semper Parata'.

Miss Carter, Miss David
  Miss Thompson, Miss Fenn,
Their knowledge in French
  we all fain would ken.

Miss Cumming, the chemist,
  herself pulled together,
And sailed through First Class,
  as light as a feather.

In every good scheme
  a comrade and fellow,
Miss Odling as strong and
  as sweet as her 'cello.

The Regent's Park Site

In 1908, with an unexpected legacy of about £11,500 from Mr J R Turle, the College Council secured the Crown lease of South Villa which was on the Inner Circle of Regent's Park. There was relief and celebration as the site seemed to be ideal for all the present needs of the College and for future development. There had been 9 acres of land with the Villa. One and a quarter acres adjoining the park lake were given to the Crown Commissioners for public use and a new 99 lease with permission for the planned buildings was obtained for the rest.

South Villa was put to use from 1909 for resident students, the Training Department and the Art School. The grounds were also pressed in to service immediately. There were fund-raising garden parties and a Botany Garden was started. In 1910 BCSA gave the Council £50 for use on South Villa grounds. They used it for levelling a number of tennis courts, there was now space for sport and relaxation.

South Villa, Regent's Park.

GRADUATION AND A NEW SITE 1909–1911

Tennis in the Grounds of South Villa.

Invitation to a Garden Party.

With the new site acquired, efforts to bring in funds for building and endowment were given greater impetus. The public were kept informed and cajoled with pamphlets and with letters in the press. The Times supported a letter of appeal with its own comments which concluded as follows.

> Happily, there is now no need to argue in favour of women's higher education. Forty years ago the case was different. People were doubtful about it, and a natural conservatism, led to many protests. A generation of experience has shown that these fears were for the most part groundless, and that the advantages of some years of well-directed study for young women largely outweigh the disadvantages.... Such higher education is, save in exceptional cases, only to be had in women's colleges, of which Bedford College is one of the most prominent. And the important point is that, owing to their late appearance on the scene, and for other causes, these colleges are heavily handicapped. Unlike the ancient foundations of Oxford and Cambridge, they have no endowments, or next to none. They have to perform a task well known to be almost impossible—to make the higher education self-supporting. Something considerable, as the appeal states, has been already done to remedy this state of things in the case of Bedford College, but much remains to be accomplished. We trust that the need so powerfully presented by the three Chancellors and their colleagues will be quickly supplied.

By the November of 1912, £129,000 had been received in the form of gifts or promises.

Arts Graduates 1910.

Science Graduates 1910.

31

EDUCATING WOMEN

REGENT'S PARK 1911–1913

Buildings were planned and the architect Basil Champney made drawings which were used in the continued appeal for funds from 1911.

There was an order to demolish South Villa but this was later rescinded. The many outbuildings were demolished, wells and ponds were filled in and work started on the new buildings in August, 1911.

The sight of these buildings going up in the park caused a lot of criticism in the newspapers about the amount of development being allowed in the Royal Park. The gift of 1¼ acres beside the lake was referred to as a 'puny sop' to the public. Questions were asked in Parliament and public meetings organised but the construction continued.

Viewed from the road in January, 1913, and nearly completed, the South Science Block is built in purple-grey brick with mouldings and dressings of red brick, on the extreme left is a corner of the Tate Library in red brick with Portland stone dressings.

Lord Eversley wrote to the Times (2.7.1913) 'permission was given in the new lease to erect the eight enormous blocks of buildings, which have now been completed and are such an eyesore and detriment to the amenity of the Park. If the public had been aware of what was being done I take it to be absolutely certain that the erection of these buildings would have been opposed and prevented'.

South Science Block seen from York Bridge Rd.

The new buildings occupied nearly the same site as the old outbuildings of South Villa and so it was unnecessary to clear away any of the trees which remained and screened the view from the public park. The new residence for students was in use for the Easter Term, 1913, but the whole complex was barely completed in time for the official opening of the new College in July, 1913.

The newly constructed Arts and Administration Building with the main entrance is seen from the road and again from the back. From the grounds the open quadrangle centres on this building topped by its clock tower. Behind the tree on the right is the South Science Block. The third side is formed by the dark stone entrance to South Villa on the far left and next to it the new North Science Block. South Villa continued in use for residence and teaching until 1930.

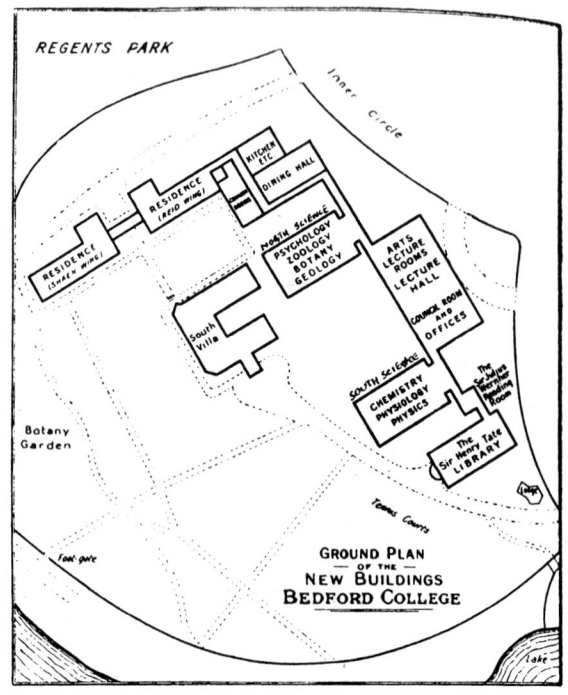

The Architect's Drawings.

REGENT'S PARK 1911-1913

The Open Quadrangle seen from the Grounds.

The Main Entrance.

South Science and Tate Library.

HALL.　　SCIENCE BLOCK.　　ARTS LECTURE ROOMS　　SCIENCE BLOCK　　LIBRARY.

EDUCATING WOMEN

ROYAL PATRONAGE AND COLLEGE PRIDE

Royal Patronage

Although the first Royal visit was in 1891 when the Empress Frederick opened the Shaen Wing in York Place, it was in 1904 that HM Queen Alexandra became the first Royal Patron of the College.

Queen Alexandra and Queen Mary were joint patrons in 1913 when they gave special sanction for emblems representative of themselves to be embodied in the new College Arms. HM Queen Mary is seen here on 4th July, 1913, accompanied by the Principal, Miss Margaret Tuke, inspecting the new buildings in Regent's Park before formally declaring them open. The College was then 64 years old.

Lilian Vass, student of English at the time enjoyed the Opening Ceremonies 'Some of us got up very early on the day and went to Covent Garden to buy cheap bunches of sweet peas. We didn't know that Queen Mary would be wearing a dress of pale pink and blue and mauve and a large hat with masses of ostrich feathers of the same colour.

'For weeks beforehand we had been practised in the court curtsey by a dancing mistress – it was very difficult. On the day we lined the

July, 1913.

June, 1955.

34

ROYAL PATRONAGE AND COLLEGE PRIDE

drive and went down in waves as Queen Mary went by. As I had my BA Inter I was entitled to wear an undergraduate gown.

'After the formal curtsey I went back to my room. I knew that it had been arranged that Queen Mary would visit one of the resident's rooms in Reid. There would be two of them in there – one was an Australian – they were to be doing their knitting.

'We were all very amused by the transformation of the garden in the days before the ceremony, suddenly there were flower borders and shrubs, rhododendrons I think, where before there had been bare earth.'

There were many subsequent occasions on which Queen Mary visited the College, sometimes informally and sometimes for special events. Her last visit was for the Centenary Celebrations in May, 1949.

HM Queen Elizabeth, the Queen Mother, visited the College in 1955 to unveil a plaque in honour of Queen Mary whom she succeeded as Patron in 1953. She met and talked with many people and is seen here in the Botany Garden talking to botany students. Subsequently the Queen Mother visited the College in Regent's Park many times to mark its special occasions and before her last visit in 1984 she expressed a wish to 'visit her own people'. In 1960 she is seen in one of the laboratories in the extension to Tuke Building which she had just officially opened.

College Pride

Bedford College was proud of those who had been its students and who in later life gained distinction in the public eye. In an account of the College in the *Universities Review*, 1905, by the Hon Mrs Bertrand Russell, a member of Council, mention is made of, amongst others, Anna Swanwick and George Elliot (Mary Ann Evans) as early pupils. Beatrice Harraden and Alice Zimmern read here for their Degrees. We had trained two of the eight women factory inspectors, Traill Christie was responsible for plague investigation in India, Sophie Bryant and Charlotte Ainslie were noted Headmistresses. We could have added to Mrs Russell's list, Madame Bodichon (Barbara Leigh-Smith) artist and feminist, Phillipa Fawcett, Educationist and Harriet Chick, Physiologist.

Coming forward from 1905 we can mention here, in addition to those on other pages, only a very small and random sample of careers and people. Until the second half of this century, the majority, particularly of the arts graduates, entered the teaching

March, 1960.

profession not only in Great Britain, as Principals of Training Colleges and Headmistresses, but also in similar positions in many other countries. Some have gained distinction in journalism and in radio and television in the direction of educational programmes and in production. Amongst authors we have Freya Stark, Margery Sharp, Phyllis Hicks and Beatrice Grimshaw. There have been chief librarians in University and other libraries, including our own Doris Bains.

In the conduct of society we note Hilda Martindale, pioneer in many positions of responsibility in Whitehall being Director of Women's Establishments at the Treasury from 1933. There were also Chairmen of the LCC and GLC; Marie Patterson, a Chairman of the TUC; Enid Lakeman, Director of the Electoral Reform Society and Mildred Ridellsdell second Permanent Secretary at the Department of Health and Social Security.

Scientists, many FRS, and those in medicine, include Helen Porter, Ethel Elderton, Maureen Young, Rosalind Pitt-Rivers, Margaret A Murray, Mary Pickford, Elizabeth Bolton, Nora Edkins and from the ranks of the early male postgraduates, David Bellamy. Prof Maureen Young wrote in 1977 in the obituary of Nora Edkins about her department and the subject of Physiology. 'The attainments of the department by the 1930s were remarkably interesting. Eighty percent of the students studying physiology separately from medicine in London University, did so at Bedford College, the failure rate was only 4%, and it was a recognised course for 2nd MB. The department provided all the staff, except the professors, at the London School of Medicine for Women, King's College of Household Science, Bedford College itself, together with about a dozen staff in Medical Schools, where women had not yet been admitted as students and a professor of physiology in a medical college in India.' 'Five of her students obtained the title of professor in medical schools, and four the distinction of FRS.' We also provided pioneers in the health and social services, the first women inspectors under the 1913 Health Act and large numbers in social welfare.

To write only of former students omits those who made a career on the staff of the College and whose scholarship has furthered their many academic subjects. College is proud of its place in the public eye and also of its role in society knowing, as Mrs Reid wrote in 1858 'that we shall never have better men till men have better Mothers'.

EDUCATING WOMEN

LIBRARY AND LECTURE ROOMS 1914

The Library

The Tate Library was built with £10,000 donated by Lady Amy Tate in memory of her husband, Sir Henry Tate, and designed by her son-in-law Mr Sydney Smith. Viewed from the grounds, the library is joined to the main teaching buildings by the single storey Wernher Reading Room.

The Tate family had long been liberal patrons of the College and often involved with the students. In 1897, resident students in York Place had enjoyed a visit to the family home in Streatham to view the collection of pictures, which Mr Tate had recently presented to the nation, before they were removed to a gallery in London.

The Tate Library was a lofty building with space for 25,000 books and about 80 readers but even from the start this was not adequate. The Wernher Reading Room provided some more space but the library was soon embarked on a continual process of building extension and room division in an effort to cope with the increase in books and students. The main library was divided into two storeys in 1932.

The six stained glass windows from the York Place Library that were a memorial to Mrs Reid donated by Miss Bostock were successfully transferred to Regent's Park. They were an elegant feature of the Sir Julius Wernher Reading Room and looked out on to the Sundial Garden.

Wernher Reading Room and Tate Library.

The Original Tate Library.

The Sundial Garden.

The Wernher Reading Room.

36

LIBRARY AND LECTURE ROOMS 1914

The Large Lecture Room

The northern corner of the open quadrangle shows the North Science Block to the left and Arts and Administration Building to the right. The windows on the far right belong to the main lecture room which became known, just as at York Place, as the 'Large'.

This lecture room occupied two storeys from ground level and with the gallery held 300 people. As well as being a teaching room, the 'Large' was the venue for inter-collegiate and public lectures and all large gatherings such as student meetings. Dr Womack, then Head of the Physics Department, was a gifted musician and a great enthusiast for Gilbert and Sullivan so the Large was used for these dramatic productions. The basement of South Villa had previously been used for dancing but when the new buildings came into use, dancing in the 'Large' during the lunch hour for the whole College became most popular even though no men partners were available.

Northern Corner of the Quadrangle.

The Science Lecture Rooms

The lecture rooms in the Science Blocks had benches for seating and in the photograph the Leitz Projector is in use to show an enlargement of a lantern slide of a microphotograph. A magazine article of 1914 about the College desribes this in detail.

Relaxing Lectures

Some of the staff took advantage of the 8 acres of grounds in the lovely summer weather to hold classes in the open air beneath the trees.

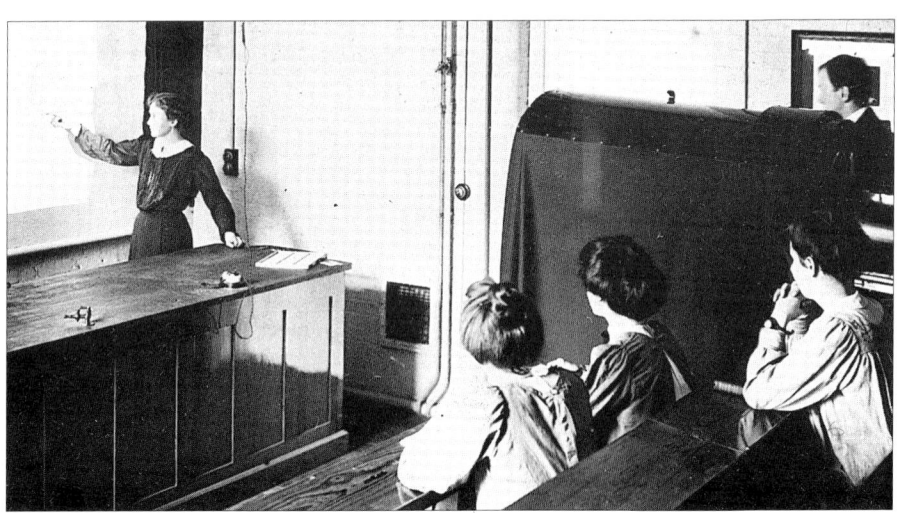

The Science Lecture Room.

The Leitz Projector uncovered.

The 'Large' Lecture Room.

A Lecture in the Grounds.

EDUCATING WOMEN

SCIENCE COURSES 1914

Lady Doctors This picture appeared in the Daily News at the end of December, 1915, captioned 'The vast war demand on the services of men doctors threatens to leave insufficient medical aid at home, but women are rapidly training to fill the gaps. The photograph shows students at Bedford College in the early stages of training. They are first year students studying the skeleton of a monkey'.

At this time, as well as having Faculties of Arts and Sciences the College was recognised for preliminary medical studies and for advanced medical studies in chemistry and physiology. The students could register at Bedford College for their initial medical training and register later at a Medical School after they had passed their examinations.

The Zoology Museum was on the top floor of North Science Block. It housed many of the specimens from the York Place Museum and there was space for the new collections that came in.

The Physiology Laboratory was on the first floor of the South Science Block. Students pose with their smoked-drum apparatus beneath the motor and pulley arrangement that served each bench.

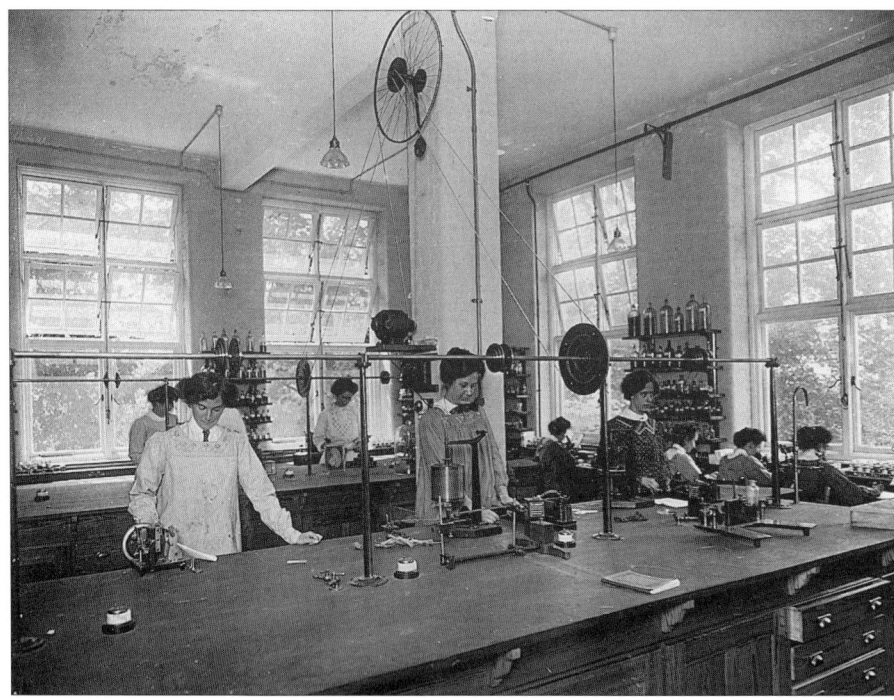

The Physiology Laboratory.

The Botany Laboratory One of the most popular studies at this time was botany. There were about fifty regular students with half of them doing the Honours Course. This view shows one of the botanical teaching laboratories on the first floor of the North Science Block where there were also staff and research rooms and a museum-library. There was another botany research suite near to the Oliver Dining Hall and this was later called the Pilcher Research Rooms. The Botany Garden in the grounds was available for studying classification and the breeding and diseases of plants. The Gardens of the Royal Botanic Society which then flourished within the Inner Circle of the park were only one minute's walk away from the Department.

The Zoology Museum.

SCIENCE COURSES 1914

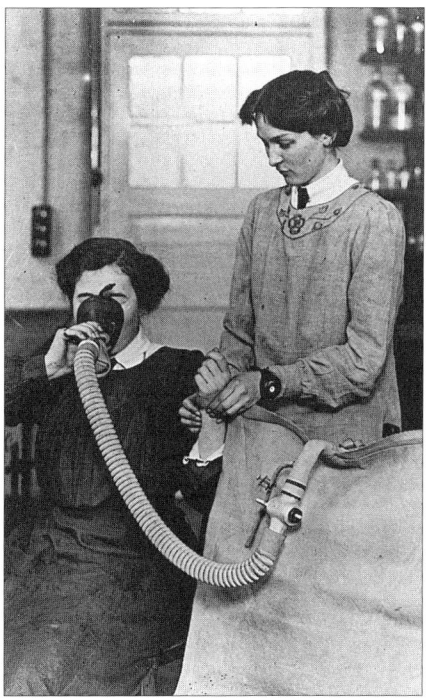

Why Weak Hearts Fail.

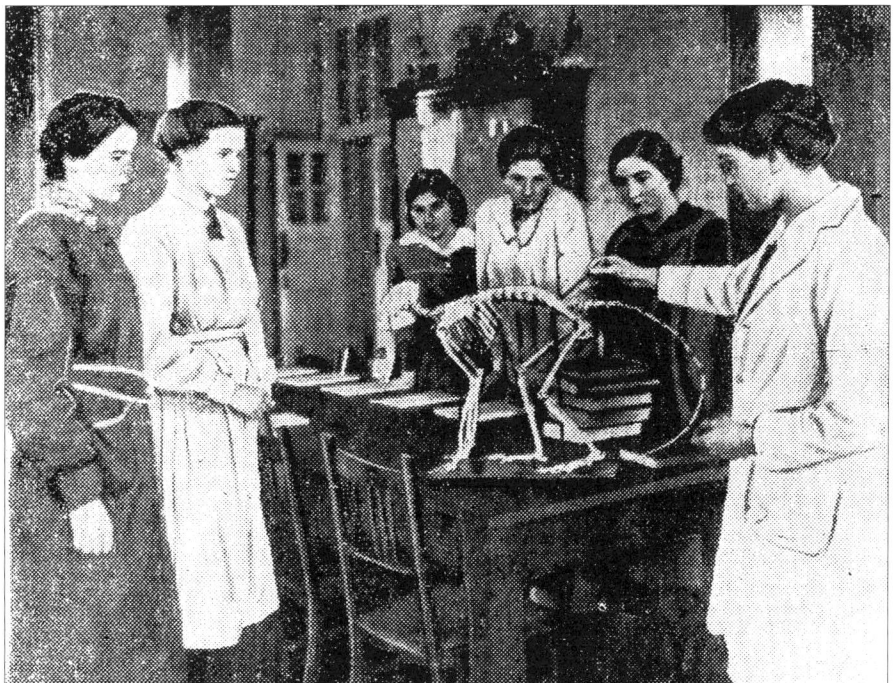

Lady Doctors.

Why Weak Hearts Fail was the caption given to this photograph of an experiment in progress. The lady breathes in to the bag; pulse and respiration rates and exhalation volume were measured both before and after running upstairs. Such experiments in human physiology were made not only by students doing Degrees in Physiology but by those doing the scientific Hygiene Course and those doing the early stages of medical training.

Mathematics and Electricity M M Partridge graduated in 1914 with an Honours Degree in Mathematics. By 1921 she had wired four English villages for electric light. She had turned herself into a Company and trained a small army of men and women workers. The villagers made their approach for electricity sometimes as a co-operative. Miss Partridge said 'nothing comes up to the thrill of the moment when they "switch on" for the first time in a village which for centuries has been dependent for its lighting on candles and oil lamps'.

The Botany Laboratory.

EDUCATING WOMEN

OLIVER DINING HALL AND COMMON ROOMS 1915

In Oliver Dining Hall at lunch time both day and resident students were served by maids who brought food from the kitchens at the side of the Hall.

At evening dinner the formal traditions of York Place were continued. A student in 1915, Margaret McDonald, tells us 'Dinner was a really ceremonial occasion. Staff and students forgathered in the Common Room and in order of precedence each chose a partner, senior offering an arm to juniors. Any fresher left over brought up the rear of the procession, sometimes with relief at not having to make conversational efforts. It was however no ordeal to be taken in to dinner by the Principal, Miss Tuke, for she had the gift of always keeping up a lively and enjoyable conversation at the high table'.

Oliver Dining Hall: View from the Gallery End.

Common Rooms

The two oak-panelled student Common Rooms were near the Dining Hall. At this period both were available to all of the students. It was here that residents gathered before dinner and coffee was served afterwards. There was a Common Room Club and in December, 1914, it reported in the Magazine. 'Students still continue to find the Common Rooms a great source of comfort and solace after their arduous tasks in other parts of the building. The Writing Room, which is available for tea-parties, is in great demand: applications for the use of it are often four deep. The popularity is greatly due to the excellence of the teas provided.'

'*Land and Water* and *The Observer* have been added this term. The Hostel, 7, Baker St, is now supplied with *The Times*, *The Daily News* and *The Westminster Gazette*. The magazines are being sent weekly to Charing Cross Hospital for the wounded.'

Oliver Dining Hall: View from the Dais.

40

OLIVER DINING HALL AND COMMON ROOMS 1915

Students in 'day dress'.

'The Common Rooms present this term a very industrious look, as few of the students taking their ease there do so without their knitting.'

Social Traditions

In general, social traditions were strong and seniors were treated with considerable respect by their juniors. We are told 'The regulations advised us to make our friends in our own year – to prevent what were known as crushes between junior and senior girls. There was a great distinction between juniors and seniors, although seniors performed many acts of kindness to freshers'. The use of Christian names was exceptional, students were mostly known by their surnames, with or without Miss, but surnames were often transformed into nicknames.

During working hours students were required to wear a jacket-suit or a dress and jacket in a dark colour or in summer a dark skirt and light blouse. For dinner they changed in to a dress and on Saturdays an evening dress was expected because there was dancing to the piano played by one of the students – Waltzes, Fox Trots, Barn-dances and Lancers.

For outside entertainment no great expenditure was necessary. Most popular with residents were visits to the theatre with a friend, particularly for matinees. Walking from College for a cup of coffee at Lyons Corner House then an hour or so queueing for a one shilling seat in the Gods and sharing a twopenny programme.

The Students Small Common Room.

The Students Large Common Room.

41

EDUCATING WOMEN

RESIDENCE, THE STUDENT UNION 1917

Residence

Only about 100 of the 400 students were able to live in the College. The new residence block comprised Reid Hall and Shaen Hall, each of these had its own entrance approached by the Residence Driveway from the Inner Circle of the park. The two Halls were joined by a corridor on the ground floor with a loggia and gallery above. One of the joys of the early days in the new residence was sleeping out in the summer term for those who liked to take the trouble to install themselves with their mattresses on this upper gallery.

The two students were snapped in 1915 with Shaen Hall in the background and South Villa to the right. There were a dozen or so residents in South Villa until 1930. More students wished to be resident than could be accommodated in College and after the move to the park, a York Place house was kept as student accommodation until 1915. In that year the only residence outside of the College was the single house, 20 Dorset Square, which held 15 students.

The end of Oliver Block, adjoining Reid Hall, housed the two student Common Rooms on the ground floor and the Principal's residence above.

A Resident Student's Room

A study bedroom in Shaen Hall. The maids had a lot of work to do in these rooms in the early years. They made the beds, fuelled the coal

Shaen Hall with the Loggia.

Reid Hall and Shaen Hall from the Residence Drive.

The Common Room-end of Oliver Block.

Corridor and Staircase in Shaen Hall.

fires and serviced the washing facilities which, apart from the bathrooms, were old-fashioned washstands with ewer and basin behind a screen in each room.

One of the first residents said 'The regulations sent to us before we came in to residence said that hair should be worn short or "up". This provided me with a problem because as a nineteen-year-old school-girl I had a long plait. I remember at the beginning of my second year a fresher came in to my room in tears begging me to put her hair up'.

'At 9.30 pm a large jug of milk and a tray of mugs was placed in each corridor. You came out of your room, chose a mug and took some milk and then sometimes arranged in whose room you would have cocoa. We provided the cocoa – you couldn't expect College to provide that – and heated up the milk on the gas ring. At 10.30 pm we were expected to be in our rooms and at 11 pm lights were to be out. In the new buildings some lights were on a pulley and you could pull your light right down and work on the floor, but the light could be seen through the glass fanlight and you could be pounced on by Miss Paterson, whose room was nearby.'

The Student Union Committee

A formal Student Union was founded only in 1913. Prior to this there had been a Senior Student and Assistants but with the move to the new buildings the Student Union was organised. Our picture shows the Union Committee 1917–1918 on the steps outside the Arts and Administration Building. The seven included the Senior Student, Miss T J Dillon second from right on back row, Treasurer, Secretary and Representatives for Science and Arts. As well as the Student Union there was by now a separate Athletic Union.

The Gate Lodge

The College Porter and his wife are shown outside their home in the hexagonal Gate Lodge at the entrance to the Library Drive. This building remains from the original South Villa.

The Student Union Committee 1917.

The Gate Lodge Mr & Mrs Morris.

A Resident Student's Room.

EDUCATING WOMEN

THE ACADEMIC WOMAN, WORLD WAR ONE

The Academic Woman

Caroline Spurgeon (1869–1942) joined the College in 1901 to teach in the Department of English, she was the author of numerous volumes of literary criticism particularly on Chaucer. In 1913 she was appointed as a Professor of the University of London to hold the Hildred Carlile Chair and to be Head in the Department of English Literature in the College. She was reported to be the first woman appointed Professor at an English University, a position she held until 1929.

The Chair was one of four, with Botany, Latin and Physics, established with part of a benefaction of £105,000 given by Sir Hildred Carlile in memory of his mother. The use of this money, in 1913, to endow Chairs was a far-sighted policy; the strength of the College depended on its power to attract first-rate scholars to its staff as well as to house them in excellent buildings.

Following the upheavals of the war and arising from her work on a British Educational Mission to America in 1918, Professor Spurgeon became in 1920, the first President of the International Federation of University Women which held its first conference in Bedford College in July, 1920.

In 1929 the Department of English Literature became the first Department in the College to have an Emeritus Professor when this distinction was awarded to Professor Spurgeon by the University.

Caroline Spurgeon.

Presentation Day

Presentation of Degrees, which had been discontinued for two years in the war, was held in the Albert Hall in May, 1919 when graduates for 1916, 1917 and 1918 were presented. A very large and successful Presentation Dinner was held at the College in the evening.

College held such a Presentation Dinner each year, with exceptions in the war-affected years 1940–48, until in the 1970s it reverted to a buffet meal as in the 1890s. Near to one of the multiple Presentation Days a buffet meal was held in the College at which the presentees were able to meet again with each other and with the staff, a pleasant annual gathering even though without the exhibitions and the music of the previous Century.

Graduates of 1917.

A Relaxation Gathering.

44

THE ACADEMIC WOMEN, WORLD WAR ONE

The War Years

College continued in the new buildings in Regent's Park throughout the four years of the war. On the whole the war seemed very remote to the students, brought home to them only by scanning the long casualty lists in the press each morning and by meetings of their own War Activities Committee. Students and staff worked together at first aid classes, held regular sessions of bandage rolling and worked at the Marylebone Women's War Club. In the long vacations of 1915 and 1916, staff of the Chemistry Department, assisted by students, prepared drugs for the Government under a scheme organised by the Royal Society.

An *Allotment Society* was formed and part of the grounds used for growing vegetables.

Relaxation Gatherings were parties for wounded soldiers held on Saturday afternoons with about 50 men each time. One Saturday it was croquet on the lawn outside Reid Hall.

The Wives and Mothers of serving men came to a party at the College and a group picture was taken in the northern corner of the quadrangle outside the Arts and Administration Building.

The Allotment Society.

Wives and Mothers.

EDUCATING WOMEN

SPACE FOR SPORT 1917-22

The move to Regent's Park meant that sports could be enjoyed in the College grounds. There was space for tennis and for practice and home matches in cricket, hockey and lacrosse. The photographs are taken in the grounds or on the lake 1917-22.

Boating became even more popular both as a sport and relaxation particularly for residents who were now nearer to the lake than when they lived in York Place. The boathouse in Regent's Park was the focus of year-round serious practice and also saw the start of the annual Scratch Race. The prizegiving after the race was held at the Boathouse and the President (Miss Tuke) or the Vice President (Prof Hilton) of the Bedford College Athletic Union officiated.

Cricket Practice outside Tate 1922.

ULAU Hockey Captain 1920-21.

1st XI Hockey 1919-20, outside 'Large' with Prof Hilton.

Tennis Courts outside Tate.

The First Tennis Pair 1917.

46

SPACE FOR SPORT 1917-22

At the Boathouse ready for the 1919 Scratch Race.

At the Scratch Race 1919.

Scratch Race Prizegiving 1921.

2nd Boat 1918, no races lost.

47

EDUCATING WOMEN

POST-WAR INCREASE IN NUMBERS 1920-26

The big increase in student numbers after the war, to 600 in 1920, meant that the buildings were over-crowded. They had been designed for only 450 students with 75 in residence. Teaching space remained inadequate throughout the 1920s. The greater variety of courses taught and the range of Societies and other activities all added to the over-crowding. Many meetings and lectures were held in the Dining Hall, tables had to be moved and the acoustics were bad. The 'Large' seated only 300, not sufficient for events such as the Principal's Inaugural Address to students which was so crowded that, as Miss Tuke wrote in 1926, 'one or two students fainted from standing in an overcrowded room'.

Residence became somewhat easier because there were now more places outside the Park. In 1919 three houses were acquired in Adamson Road, Swiss Cottage, using contributions collected by former students and they housed 37 students. In 1915 the College had just one house in Dorset Square, No 20 with 15 students. By 1925 there were four adjacent houses, Nos 35-38 with 59 students, and in that year the residences were re-named and given brass name plates for their doors. Adamson Road Hostel became Bedford College House and Dorset Square Hostel became Notcutt House after Rachel Notcutt (1841-1921) who had been a student, librarian, resident in the Boarding House, friend and counsellor to students and a Reid Trustee.

The ex-Army Huts

The Chemistry Department had outgrown its laboratories on the top floor of S Science Block. The Council reported that it was 'quite impossible to accommodate all the new students who desire to take up chemistry or even all the senior students who desire to qualify for an Honours Degree'. The Department expanded in to temporary ex-army huts placed in the quadrangle outside S Science. The huts were erected in 1919 and removed in 1930. The van is bringing chemical supplies to the huts via the Library Drive.

An aerial view of the College in 1921 shows the temporary huts in the quadrangle and South Villa still standing at the end of the N Science Block.

POST-WAR INCREASE IN NUMBERS 1920-26

Staff of the 1920s.

The Staff

Grouped on the library steps are just over half of the teaching staff of the mid-1920s. The number of staff was increasing and in these years general countrywide attention was first being paid to comparability of salaries, pensions and conditions of service for academic staff. The Association of University Teachers held its first annual meeting at Bedford College in June 1920; the President gave comparative figures and said that the underpaid condition of the members of the assistant staffs of the Universities was shocking.

The College was a pioneer who had achieved respected status and its members, knowledgeable in the field of women's education, often served, advised and helped in other educational battles.

In 1922 the London Hospital caused a furore when it decided on the advice of the London Medical School to take no more women students and revert to its old custom of training only men 'not because they objected to the medical education of women but because of the difficulties which arose in a mixed school of men and women students'. Other hospitals followed this lead. The University of London set up a Committee in 1928 to look at this problem of medical education for women. The two women on the Committee were the Principal, Margaret Tuke, and Ethel Strudwick, a former student and staff member of Bedford College and High Mistress of St Paul's Girls School

S Villa and N Science with the N end of the huts.

Ex-army Huts in the Quadrangle.

Chemistry Laboratory in S Science Block.

EDUCATING WOMEN

A WIDER RANGE OF ACTIVITIES 1920–26

During this period many of the subjects taught in College developed along new lines and there were far more courses available. Well established subjects developed new activities.

The 'Internationals' and the Nursing Connection

The courses for International Students started in 1921 at the request of the League of Red Cross Societies and were later under the auspices of the Florence Nightingale International Foundation. One course trained nurses for posts in Public Health, another was intended for Nurse Administrators and Tutors in Schools of Nursing. The students came each year from 10–20 different countries and over the years 42 countries were represented, a residence was provided for them in Manchester Square by the British Red Cross Society. The courses ended with the start of the Second World War.

The course in Scientific Hygiene (1895–1918), which had now given way to courses in Social Studies and training courses for Social Work, had equipped the College for the teaching of Internationals which covered the scientific, sociological and economic aspects of nursing. Medical Sociology continued to be an interest in the College and it was well represented as a research subject in the modern Department of Sociology which had teaching links with a number of London Medical Schools. In the 1980s the College offered undergraduate courses leading to BSc in Nursing Studies.

Another continuing connection with nursing came from the fact that ever since the move to Regent's Park the College had provided premises and residence for vacation courses, conferences and meetings; organisations often returned year after year for their annual gatherings. Prominent amongst the regulars were societies of Matrons and Sister Tutors and the Institute of Midwives held its Jubilee Celebrations (1930–31) and National and International Congresses (1950s) in College.

The Sargent Laboratory

The Sargent Laboratory was built using a legacy from Alice Sargent and opened by her brother Lord Justice Sargent. Alice was an early student of the College and a member of Council from 1901–1909. The laboratory was a welcome addition to crowded research and teaching space, it was attached to

The International Students, their Staff and Miss Tuke 1921.

The International Students, their Staff and Miss Jebb 1932.

South Science Block.

A WIDER RANGE OF ACTIVITIES 1920–26

the greenhouses in the Botany Garden and thus near to good growing conditions for the plants. The legacy enabled the Department to develop its work in plant physiology.

Field Work in the Sciences developed strongly at this time. The Department of Geology favoured the Isle of Arran in Scotland. Here, at Easter 1926, Professor Leonard Hawkes is with his students outside the cottages at Glen Sheraig where they are cleaning their boots ready for the work of the day.

Graduates' Associations
In Baker Street, the Bedford College Students Association (BCSA) had involved both present and past students and the College Magazine had recorded their activities. In Regent's Park the current students formed the Student Union and the Bedford College Magazine (1886–1913) was replaced by the Bedford College Union Magazine. From 1921, present students were no longer automatically members of BCSA and so it came to involve mainly graduates. It transformed for a period to BCOSA and then from 1963 to BCA, Bedford College Association. Under the different names it has continued from 1894 to be the medium through which all past students and staff could act as a helpful force in the affairs of the College.

A play, produced in 1920 which was entirely the work of graduates was entitled *DITHIRADNE IN LACRIMIS*. It was a burlesque of Greek tragedy written in English verse by three ex-students. The College had been well-known for its productions of authentic Greek plays and the national press always reviewed them. Likewise with this production which was very well received. We read, 23.2.1920, Daily Telegraph: 'Their miniature tragedy, which deals with the inadvertent murder of a pet cat, might stand as a light hearted but complete illustration of the principles contained in Aristotle's "Poetics".' ... and Morning Post: 'Ancient and solemn mysteries reduced to laughter-provoking absurdity!'

The figure at the centre back of the group is Miss Norah McNaulty who was a student in 1912–1915, in 1916 she joined the College administration and was Registrar 1945–62. She was present at the last College Reunion held in Regent's Park in 1985.

Residence and Boating
Dorothy Chapman (later Mrs Griffiths), studying mathematics, 1924–27, and resident in Notcutt House writes:– 'Once a week we were issued with six pennies to work this gas heated geyser for our baths or any hot water that we needed. This was remarkably inadequate a penny bath was by no means hot enough and we were supposed to make the six pennies do and not add pennies of our own. We were thus reduced to 3 baths a week. My room mate, Katharine needed more for she was a keen boater and given to falling in. The lake had just as many wild fowl then as now and it smelt horrid. So she needed baths and her clothes were a problem when they needed to be dried.

'We had half-an-hour boating practice about twice a week and the use of the boathouse on the little island on the lake. A boatman and his son looked after the boats and were presumably paid by the sixpences which we paid for our boating tickets.

'At first we had fixed seats and when we had mastered this, sliding seats which made us go faster and were less laborious. We had big safety pins with which we tried to pin our skirts in to shorts which would keep them out of the works of the sliding seats. Shorts were introduced at some time along the line and I collected the discarded boating skirts and turned them into school tunics for the Guides in my Guide Company who were very keen to have tunics to wear in school as they were a great status symbol.'

The Opening of the Sargent Laboratory in the Botany Garden 9th July, 1925.

Geology Field Work in Arran.

Boaters 1922.

Graduates' Dramatic Production 1920.

EDUCATING WOMEN

UNIONS AND UNIFORM 1920s

Unions

The Student's Handbook, 1923-24 gives the College Colours as 'green, grey, brown and yellow. Green and grey are Minerva's colours. Brown and yellow are respectively the Arts and Science colours of the University'. Bedford College Athletic Union, BCAU formed 1913, controlled the Sports Clubs and the use of the official College sports girdle and the blazer both in green with grey edging. As competitive team sports increased over the years BCAU was active in prompting the College to acquire a sports ground. In 1922 a sum was raised by bazaars and entertainments and a ground bought at Northolt near Ruislip. The Air Ministry made a compulsory purchase of that in 1925 and then the College bought the ground at Headstone Lane near Pinner with facilities for hockey, lacrosse and cricket.

The BC Students' Handbook for Session 1923-24 tells students – 'The University of London Union Society was formed in March, 1921, with the aim of bringing about a closer co-operation between the Colleges and Schools of the University and of representing the students of the University of London in their relations with other student organisations throughout the world'.

ULU gave a Garden Party, its first public social gathering, at Bedford College in June, 1921. It already had a membership of 1,200 and was negotiating for premises.

The University of London Athletic Union – Women's Branch, was much older than ULU. It organised inter-collegiate matches and set up ULAU teams to represent the University; it had its own uniforms and awarded University colours. Participation in ULAU enhanced the pride in BCAU.

In 1920 the Bedford College Boating Club had a membership of 360 out of a total of 600 students. From the Council Report 1927-28 'On the side of Athletics the students have done particularly well this year. In Boating the College heads the lake, and in other sports she holds the Intercollegiate Cups for Tennis, Cricket and 2nd XI Hockey'.

The College Song

M M Haslan a student of chemistry tells us 'this song was sung heartily by us at College between 1917 and 1921'. The subjects mentioned refer back to the days in York Place.

Lacrosse 1st XI 1924-25.

Cricket XI 1926 with Prof Hilton Vice-President Athletic Union.

Hockey 1st XI 1923 or 24. Winners of the University Hockey Cup.

UNIONS AND UNIFORM 1920s

'In days of old when men to men
In Colleges expounded
The women might not learn a thing –
'Twas then BC was founded.
So let us all with one accord
Pursue this way to knowledge
The jolliest, sweetest, surest way
The way of Bedford College.

So all who yearn to be BAs
And all who science favour
Who paint or sing or do hygiene
And work with pleasure flavour.
Now let us all with one accord
Pursue this way to knowledge
The jolliest, cheeriest, sweetest way
The way of Bedford College.'

Regulations about Uniform
From the report of the Council for Session 1919–20 – 'Since January, 1920, it has been made compulsory for students to wear Academic Dress when attending lectures and at public functions. This innovation was made in compliance with a strong wish expressed by the students. The Council received a deputation, heard both sides of the question and decided to make the desired regulation.'

Extracts from 'General Information' in the Students Handbook 1923–24:

Academic Dress to be worn on all public occasions; consists of cap and gown, to be worn over a white dress

College Boats 1926.

Academic Dress on a Public Occasion – outside the peeling paintwork of South Villa awaiting the Princess Royal June, 1927.

or navy coat and skirt, black shoes and stockings and white gloves.

Gowns must be worn by students at lectures, general meetings and on all public occasions except when working in the Science Blocks and Army Huts. The first infringement of this rule must be reported to the Union Committee. Fines will be imposed of 1/- for the second and 2/6 for the third and subsequent offences.

Hats Students may not go out of the College grounds without hats on, except to and from the Boat House before 10 am.

Tunics may not be worn in College without a long coat except when going to and from games.

Smoking Students may smoke in the Small Common Room, between 12 and 3 p m, and afterwards when the room is not engaged for tea. Students engaging the room may smoke after tea. Students may not smoke in the garden except on the path round residence after dinner.

The Mortar Board
A number of newspapers carried the following item in Feb 1927. '"To Go or Not to Go" the fate of the "Mortar Board" discussed at Bedford College. The debate on the "Mortar Board" for women is raging in all women's colleges where it is worn. With long hair, state its opponents, it cannot be made to fit, and with a shingle or Eton crop it fits the head like an egg-cup fits the egg. In many colleges the cap is worn only on state occasions.'

BOATING

(How is the glory departed from the lake !)

Those early mornings of long ago !
Crisp and cold, and the mists still low,
When we issued forth from the little gate
And crossed the bridge at a martial rate—
Lordly Cox, deferential Crew—
To learn all the things a boat could do.
Beginning as Freshers in wallowing tubs,
With oars turning cartwheels on rowlock hubs,
And finding as foreign as Persian or Greek
The correct boating jargon we tried to speak,
Working up, thro' torts and incredible feats
To the low, slim racers with sliding seats.
(And decorous boatmen averted their gaze
While we dealt with the skirts
Which obtained in those days,
Hoisting them up with safety pins three,
One in the middle and one at each knee.)
Then back with the speed which appetite brings
(Past the statuesque cormorant drying his wings)
To the breakfast so dear to a hungry crew,
And ready to sample a lecture or two.
And College Races became the thing
With crowded banks and excitement high,
The flashing blades and the rhythmic cry,
And the arrowy winner shooting by—
(Races lesser in very minute degree
Than one which we hear about annually,
When obscure universities row from Putney.)
O memories crowd on thick and fast
When a hundredth birthday comes at last,
And perhaps we regret above all, in truth,
The incredible energies of our youth.

AN OLD STUDENT (1921–24)

From the Centenary Issue Bedford News, 1949.

EDUCATING WOMEN

RAISING FUNDS 1919–27

The Need for Funds

As in 1888 and in 1903 so again in 1919 a Committee was formed to appeal for funds, this time under the Chairmanship of Sir Hildred Carlile. The Extension and Endowment Appeal aimed for more teaching buildings, more residence and for endowments for the library and other academic work. In asking for money, stress was laid on the impetus to women's education given by a variety of causes but particularly the position created by the war and the enfranchisment of women. As well as direct appeal there were the well-tried garden fetes, dramatic productions and celebration dinners.

Each summer from 1920 to 1924 the complex organisation of an English Garden Party went in to full swing with military bands and a variety of entertainments in the grounds, or inside if wet. HRH Princess Mary, The Princess Royal, came to the College on a number of these occasions and is seen here on her way to a 'Pastoral Performance of Pelleas and Melisanda' in June, 1923.

The money collected in the early years of the appeal was spent in minor building changes but the College administration and the Building Committee had been busy planning the best site and structure for the major development. The final plan was for a building to join the ends of North and South Science Blocks and so to close the quadrangle. £110,000 were needed and with £66,000 in hand work was commenced. On 9th June, 1927, HRH Princess Mary performed the ceremony of laying the foundation stone of this building.

At the Garden Party, June, 1923.

Pride and Prejudice

On 24th March, 1922, at the Palace Theatre there was a matinee performance of *Pride and Prejudice* in aid of the Appeal. Radiant with legend and memory, Ellen Terry who was born in the year that the College was founded, had a stupendous walk-on part. She appeared as a guest at Mr Bingley's Ball and danced the Sir Roger de Coverley – all for Bedford College. Others in the cast were Mary Jerrold, May Whitty, Ivor Novello, Viola Tree and Ben Webster. The matinee, in the presence of HM Queen Mary made a profit of £800.

The Foundation Stone

The laying of the Foundation Stone was well covered in the press. Five national papers published a letter furthering the Appeal.

'This will be a memorable occasion in the history of the College. The war quickened the already growing demand for higher education for women, and the great desire of women for improved scientific training has made the need for a new science wing imperative, more especially as some of the temporary wooden huts in which some of the science work is carried on have been condemned, and must now be replaced with a permanent structure.

'At this moment when it appears probable that the younger women may shortly become enfranchised, it is of the first importance that as many as may desire it should have the opportunity for higher education, with its broadening and steadying effect

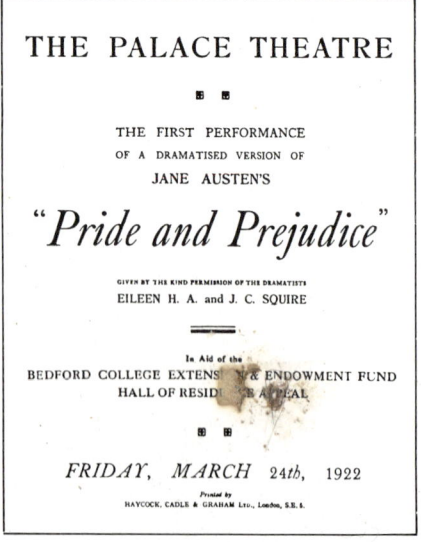

Star-studded Drama For the Residence Appeal.

Presentation Day 1926.

Studying Outside South Villa 1927.

54

upon mind and character. We appeal with confidence ....'

The Sunday Express 29.5.1927 noted 'Next week Princess Mary will lay the foundation stone of the new science wing that has become necessary because of the growing desire on the part of the girls of to-day – those pleasure seeking, cocktail-taking, and dancing-mad young women – for improved scientific training.'

The ceremony was to be broadcast and this entailed extra arrangements such as the large microphone seen hanging beside the foundation stone, and also preliminary notice in a number of papers 'When Princess Mary (Viscountess Lascelles) lays the foundation stone of the new wing of Bedford College for Women this afternoon the ceremony will be relayed to London and Daventry and broadcast from 2LO and from the Plymouth station.'

The Manchester Guardian 10.6.1927 concerned itself with what lay below the stone. '.... showed her the box that was to be placed beneath it. It contained a copy of a London newspaper, a copy of the College magazine, specimen coins of the year, and photographs of the president and committee of the College Union. With the exception of the photographs, which will show investigators of some distant century the fashions worn by more or less earnest women of to-day this collection seemed to some of the guests singularly unimaginative and uninteresting.

'A few cuttings might well have been included reporting the fact that a woman had won the Newdigate Prize, that a woman aviator had made a non-stop flight from London to Scotland, that Oxford feared its overthrow by women, and so on. A vanity bag completely equipped should certainly have been included, a bargain sale advertisement, and a list of openings for women with average salaries. The record would be incomplete without some newspaper correspondence on the faults and failing of the modern girl and the impropriety of allowing her to vote at twenty-one.'

In 1981, Gwyneth Pye, née Jenkins, present at the ceremony as a student, wrote 'there was a strong spirit of hope in the future: the terrible aftermath of the Great War had been overcome and for women in particular there seemed very bright prospects, ... So the laying of the Foundation Stone ... was a joyful and carefree occasion'.

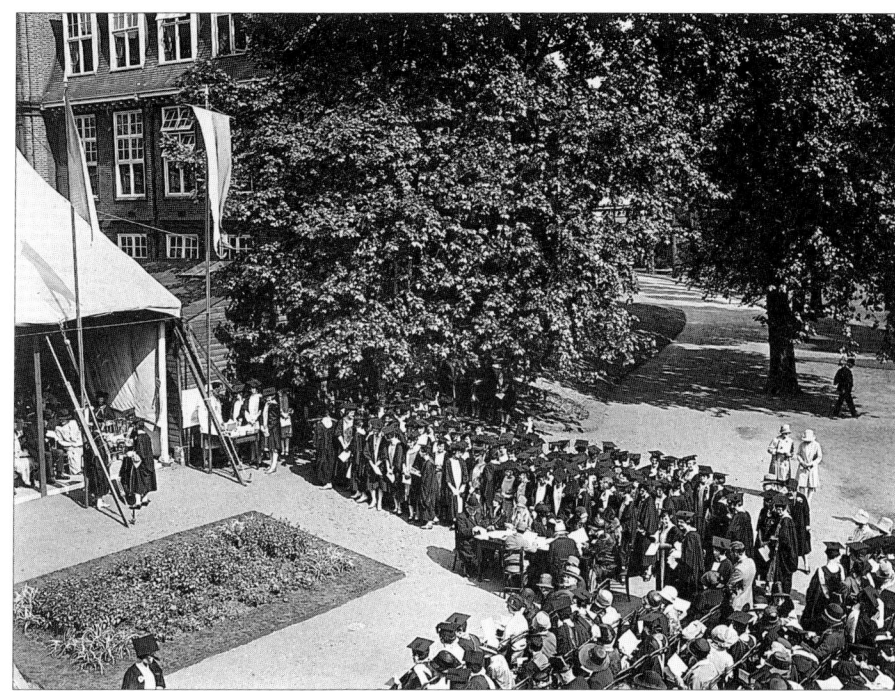
Spectators with S Science in the Background.

Applying Mortar for the Stone-laying.

Refreshments after the Foundation Stone Ceremonies.

EDUCATING WOMEN

THE TUKE BUILDING 1930

The Building

Miss Margaret Tuke, later Dame Margaret, had become Principal in 1907 and she left that office in December, 1929. The new building, the planning and financing of which she had steered through the last ten years, was named after her. The Council felt that this was a fitting tribute to her great work. All the College buildings at that time, old and new, were the result of her inspiration having been conceived, designed and built during her 22½ years as Principal. The architect of the Tuke Building was Maxwell Ayrton.

Work started on the South Wing in 1927. The South Wing and the Central block, that completed the quadrangle, were occupied in January, 1930, and proved to be 'very satisfactory' for the departments that moved in. The New Hall, later called the Tuke Hall, could seat 650. It was used for examinations in the summer term of 1930. In 1929 a major annual College lecture was endowed in memory of Dame Millicent Fawcett, the subject to relate to 'Changes in the position of women in the last 100 years'. The first lecture in October, 1930, might well have been given in the New Hall.

The huts in the quadrangle were demolished at Easter, 1930, and the new turf for the quadrangle was purchased from the students' Athletic Ground. In the summer of 1930, South Villa was demolished with great difficulty as it had been so well built. On the freed site the North Wing was built and joined to the Central block. The North Wing, seen in construction behind its scaffolding, was ready for occupation from October, 1931.

The Funds

The Extension and Endowment Committee worked very hard during 1930 and 1931 to clear the debts incurred from the new building. The students presented a pageant at a Garden Party in May, 1930 to raise some money. Called 'Time's Daughters' and written by a former student it followed the evolution of the 'Girl of 1930' from the suppressed woman of earlier ages. Played with enthusiasm to 1,500 guests, in excellent costumes and in lovely summer weather, it made £680 for the Appeal. A Festival Dinner with 150 guests was held in Lincoln's Inn Hall in December, 1930 in the presence of HRH Prince George and £2,818 was collected.

The South Wing Viewed from the Library.

Construction of the North Wing Oct 1930–Mar 1931.

The New Chemistry Laboratory in Tuke Building.

THE TUKE BUILDING 1930

The Astronomical Observatory

The dome of the Astronomical Observatory can be seen above the north-east corner of the Central block. The Observatory was opened by the Astronomer Royal in March, 1930, seen here at the telescope. This is a 7 inch equatorial refractor telescope built in 1872 by the famous firm of Grubb in Dublin. It had been commissioned by the Royal Artillery Institution at Woolwich and was built for £500, its purpose being the training of young officers in astronomy. By 1926 it was little used at Woolwich and was presented to the College.

The Opening

The formal opening of the Tuke Building was performed in the New Hall by HM Queen Mary on 24th June, 1931. Her Majesty then toured the whole building, met the Heads of 7 newly-accommodated Departments and inspected the special displays in the Departments of Social Studies, Psychology, Geography and Chemistry as thoroughly, no doubt, as the Shaen Wing had been inspected 40 years previously. After tea Her Majesty met some of the men who had been involved in the construction and later joined a general Garden Party in the grounds. The guests were then free to tour the building including the basement which housed cloakrooms, Engineer's workshop and messrooms and cloakrooms for laboratory attendants and domestic staff. Tea served on the Quadrangle terrace sustained them for the tour.

The Completed Building showing the Observatory Dome.

A Canopy on the Quadrangle Terrace.

The Astronomer Royal with Students and Telescope.

At the Garden Party 24th June, 1931.

EDUCATING WOMEN

THE EARLY 1930s

The Gates
The decorative gates, designed by Maxwell Ayrton, were placed on the Main, Residence and Library Drives in 1931. They were donated by Henrietta Busk and after her death in 1936 became a memorial to her.

The Tuke Hall
The 'New Hall' was used continually. During this decade there was a heavy programme in College of series of public lectures, special University lectures and week-end and vacation conference meetings.

The Dramatic Society now had a proper stage on which to perform. In June 1930, it was reported in the Magazine. 'The new stage has given the Dramatic Society a setting worthy of its importance and experience. Its drop scenes, side-curtains, devices for entrance and exit were marvellous compared with the make-shifts of the "Large", but the acting of "The Shoemaker's Holiday" passed beyond dependence on mere stage equipment.' There were one or two major productions by the Society each year.

Hindsight on the 1930s
Dame Margaret Miles was a student in the early 1930s, she gave us these comments in 1985. 'If you look back at pre-war Bedford, the secret of its success and its spirit lay in its size and the powerful Principals and top administrators – Miss Tuke, Miss Jebb, Miss Monkhouse, Miss Haydon. All strong, dedicated people who stayed for a long time. They created a good human spirit.'

'I had to pledge myself to be a teacher in order to obtain a 4-year Board of Education grant (for most students it was their parents or scholarships that paid the fees, etc) and then had to work as a teacher for three years at least in a maintained school.

'All women in higher education were part of an elite then. We were nearly all from middle class families, living in a boarding school type of atmosphere. But there was a good, free liberal spirit. It was all female, but no one had the notion that "women worked better when men weren't around". As a Governor I was in favour of admitting men when the time came but with hindsight I can see that it changed the nature of the College and put it in direct competition with the large multi-faculty Colleges – a competition it could not win.'

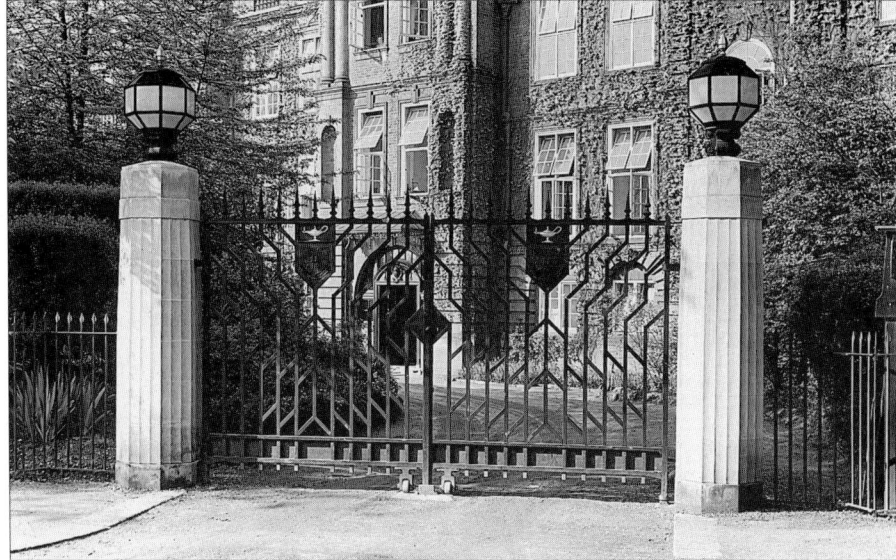
The Busk Memorial Gates.

An Academic Audience in the New Hall.

1934 A production of Berkeley Square in the New Hall.

THE EARLY 1930s

The Library

The Reid Memorial Windows in the Wernher Reading Room still gave the students a view out on to the Sundial garden. The College gardens had taken time to recover from the neglect of the war years. Since 1922 Miss Alice Lindsell had been the honorary Garden Curator in charge of the gardeners and she had brought about marked improvements.

The library was growing at the rate of 2,000 volumes per year and in 1932 the main Tate Library was divided horizontally to give a stack room below and leaving the upper library still 18ft high. In the alcove on the end wall of the upper library is the terracotta figure of the Angel Gabriel. This angel came to symbolise the library for generations of students and, unlike the Reid windows, it survived the bombing of 1941.

From the Bedford College Union Magazine.

Upper Tate Library.

Pigeon-Holes.

Lecture.

Wernher Reading Room.

Oliver.

Boating.

Prof Hilton (Mathematics) and students using the telescope 1931.

59

EDUCATING WOMEN

THE MID 1930s

A Garden Party

In brilliant sunshine on Thursday, 6th July 1933, students, their parents and friends were at a Garden Party in the College grounds. Amongst the guests were the Earl of Athlone, Chancellor of the University, his wife HRH Princess Alice, the Mayoress of St Marylebone and the member of Parliament for the University.

Students and Women Staff

The Small Oliver Common Room was now reserved for students who lived in one or other of the College Residences; this was the room which became the post-graduate Common Room in the 1950s. The Large Oliver Common Room, which was available to all students, now had a framed bas-relief over the chimneypiece. 'The Labourers in the Vineyard' was presented to the College in 1923–24 by the sculptor Margaret M Giles.

The proportion of women on the teaching and research staff of the College had risen from 57% in 1912–13 to 65% in 1922–23 and now in the mid 1930s it hovered just below this last figure. By 1952–53 it was 50% and in 1982–83 was down to 29%.

Students' Large Common Room with 'The Labourers in the Vineyard'.

Sport

Boating was still an exceedingly popular activity. It centred, as since 1889, on the Regent's Park Boathouse and the lake. The annual College races on the lake brought out a large and enthusiastic crowd of student followers on the bank.

Mary Harrop (née Mostyn) tells us 'Freshers were allocated to 2nd or 3rd year students for training in tubs, rather unwieldy boats for two people plus a cox. From there one graduates to outriggers which were narrower and lighter and used for racing. We used to train for the annual bumps and races in both outriggers and skiffs.

'Before anyone was allowed to race they had to obtain a medical certificate of fitness. The test for this was: pulse rate taken, then run up the

Garden Party, July 1933.

60

THE MID 1930s

Following the Boat Races 1932.

stairs to the top of Reid Residence and down again, which was timed, then the pulse taken a second time. According to the result one obtained a full or half certificate or none. For racing a full certificate was needed.' We know that the same tests were done on the stairs in Notcutt House in the mid 1920s.

'A dongola was a punt, used with canoe paddles and raced for fun in College. The students at the front of the (pictured) dongola won College Colours for winning races against Queen Mary's College or Reading University which, I believe, were the only two which had women's crews in or near London.'

Technical Assistance in Laboratories

The smooth running of the laboratories for both teaching and research was ensured by the well-nigh indispensable services of experienced technical staff such as those pictured in 1932. The provision of this help had developed over the last twenty years. In 1911 one Head of a Science Department had had to struggle with a reluctant Council for permission to employ a part-time laboratory boy to assist in two departments. Back in 1903 science students sometimes contacted the 'workshop' for help but we think this was the building-maintenance workshop and nothing akin to the science workshop which was developed in College in the 1950s to back up the fully-trained departmental technical staff of more recent decades.

The Dongola beside the Island in the Park Lake 1936.

Chief Technicians in the Science Departments 1932.

EDUCATING WOMEN

THE LATE 1930s AND EVACUATION

Roberts

In 1938 the Senior Porter, Mr Gustave William Roberts retired after service with the College since 1902. He reflected on the change from the earlier students who were 'quite ladies' and looked charming in their long sweeping skirts, to the present students of 1938, just as charming with their free and easy ways and their enthusiasm. Asked about his ideal Professor, Mr Roberts said it was 'the one who gave the least trouble'.

Celebrations

To celebrate the year of the Coronation of King George VI, the College held an evening 'Reception to Old Students' on 3rd July, 1937. There was music and refreshments for the 1,500 who attended and the College rooms were open including the Library and Observatory. Great efforts were made to contact all old students, efforts not repeated until 1985.

Commemoration – of the founding of the College – first took its latter-day style in 1938 when there was an oration in College followed by a dinner at the Senate House. After this, with a gap from 1939 to 1950, annual commemoration events were held through to the 1960s; in 1956 a garden party tea, in 1957 a tea and oration followed by a dinner in College for the dignitaries and just some of the staff and students.

Roberts at the Main Entrance 1935.

Mr G W Roberts 1938.

The 'Large' viewed from N Science.

From the BC Union Magazine June 1938.

62

THE LATE 1930s AND EVACUATION

Evacuation

Evacuation of the College away from central London was inevitable in the autumn of 1939 with the outbreak of the Second World War. Cambridge was the final destination and the University there tried to smooth the trauma for uprooted departments and students needing somewhere to live. Members of the College administration are pictured outside 'Springfield', Sidgwick Avenue, Cambridge which became the address of the College. The house had been previously the home of Miss Geraldine Jebb, the Principal, and became the administration headquarters of the evacuated College.

Springfield, Cambridge.

Professor Dorothy Tarrant, Head of the Department of Greek tells us – 'When war broke out on September 3rd, 1939, a party of volunteers were already busy dealing with the Library; the Tate and other reading-rooms were cleared, a working collection of books removed with us to Cambridge, two consignments of valuable volumes stored in country places, and the rest piled up in the Stack Room behind blast walls. In Cambridge, houses were secured for the Library, for Arts tutorial and seminar rooms and for the Union Society; lectures were provided for in Newnham or University premises, while the Science departments doubled-up more or less comfortably with their opposite numbers in the University laboratories. The problems of transport may be imagined, at a time of general confusion; and altogether there was immense work, for the Administrative Staff especially. Billeting was a formidable task. Some students dropped away for various reasons, but about 430 came to Cambridge and all had to be lodged. One house was run as a very small hostel, in which Matron had her sick-bay. The Cambridge residents proved kind and hospitable, and many lasting friendships were formed. Miss Cullis (then Resident Tutor) was the first Billeting Officer, succeeded after a year by Miss Crewdson. There was a uniform billeting fee, paid through the College, so that for the time being everyone and yet no one was "resident". The Staff found their own lodging; a few brought their families and made homes, while some others carried on amphibiously between Cambridge and London.

'A premature return home in 1940 was followed by the onset of heavy raids upon London; so back we went again, and again billets had to be found. In course of time many changes were necessary in these and in our other premises, and we became more and more scattered over Cambridge. Most people took to bicycling, and careered around hazardously in true Cambridge fashion, enjoying meanwhile all the beauties of the place.

'The Union Society carried on in three successive homes, borrowing a large lecture-room for General Meetings. For athletics, Newnham hospitably allowed the use of their field and courts; swimming and boating (mostly informal) were enjoyed. Freshers' Socials and College dances were held at that hub of Cambridge society, the Dorothy Café. The sectional societies rather tended to merge with their Cambridge equivalents, to which Bedford people were made welcome. Work, too, became partly inter-collegiate and we were admitted to the University Library. The scientists again did valuable work for the war effort. The Intermediate and Finals examinations were held in halls at Newnham; results were pretty well up to standard, in spite of conditions and of the call-up which interfered with many people's courses. Canteen work, landwork and other voluntary service was freely taken up, and fire-watching on our various premises was provided on an elaborate rota system. There were many alarms and some raids.

'The main problem at Cambridge was to keep up our unity as a College; we met in our own groups, but never all together. As some remedy for this, a ceremonial College Assembly (held in the Guildhall) was instituted in October, 1941. It was repeated the next two years and once in the New Hall after our return home.'

The staff and students of the English Department organised a party of the Reid Society in May, 1941, at Burrell's Field, Cambridge. The Reid Literary Society was one of the oldest and most respected of the Bedford College Societies.

Staff of the English Department at the Reid Society Party.

Voluntary Landwork; Fruitpicking at Rolfe's Farm, Wickhambrook, 1940.

EDUCATING WOMEN

LONDON AND THE BOMBING 1941

War-time Tenants

Some Bedford College Staff remained at Regent's Park, particularly the Bursar's, maintenance and kitchen staff, to look after the various tenants who lived there or used the buildings. There was a hostel for civil servants and, for a time, the Women's Voluntary Service ran an evacuation nursery in the residence. There were two longer term tenants: the Dutch Government in exile and the foreign transcription service of the BBC.

The Bombing

On Saturday, 10th May, 1941, in one of the last and worst of the great air raids on London about one third of the College buildings in the park were wrecked beyond hope of repair by high explosive and incendiary bombs.

Notcutt House in Dorset Square was also severely damaged. Some graphic accounts of that night in the College have been preserved, particularly one by Mr A A Cooper, the handyman who with others, from both Bedford and the BBC, tried to save the buildings. This was a heart-breaking and hopeless task when the water supplies failed and when no fire engine could come until the next morning because of all the damage in the rest of London.

Quoting from Mr Cooper's account – 'There was little anyone could do now, the fire everywhere was a blazing furnace. Oliver Hall was nearly gutted, but fortunately the wind changed, saving (the rest of) Oliver Building and the Residential Building. Wiffen and I tried the nearest hydrant in the Circle, but this was off also.

'The next I remember was some of the women returning for warmer clothes. Things were now a little quieter overhead, and the women's first concern was to make tea for all of us. Later, I noticed all the women both staff and domestic, working hard, bringing the food stores salvaged from the kitchen round to Tuke kitchen, also making the tennis court outside Shaen Hall a food dump which they shifted later! ....'

And in conclusion, speaking for himself and the other College maintenance man .... 'Lastly, Wiffen and I think that we both felt the defeat more than did Mr Mortimer and his men (from the BBC). Right from the beginnings of the war we have been standing by for anything that may occur in a raid, after all we knew the building, it was our job to

WVS Evacuation Nursery in the Residence.

Arts and Administration and N Science with Oliver in the Background.

LONDON AND THE BOMBING 1941

try and defeat anything .... A great deal of the College is still standing and I sincerely hope with all College servants that it will continue to do so until all this madness is over, proving that the life's devotion of those who had built it up from the beginning has not been in vain.'

The Damage

The pictures show the main damage to the buildings. The single-storey Pilcher Research Rooms were completely destroyed, they are in the foreground of the burnt out shell of Oliver Dining Hall with the apsed, dais end nearest to us.

Viewed from the S Science Block across the quadrangle, the Arts and Administration building is to the right with its upper floors gutted and the firemen still hosing them down. North Science Block on the far side of the quadrangle was completely gutted. The view of the Main Entrance does not reveal the amount of damage to this building which was obvious from the quadrangle.

One bomb exploded in the grounds outside Tuke Building, fortunately far enough away not to demolish it. The fire brigade continued to damp the fires for the whole of the next day. The College kitchen staff, after salvaging food stores all night, continued to serve meals to everyone concerned and the maintenance staff salvaged what they could and helped to dampen fires.

The National Union of Students

In the summer of 1941 Mary Corsellis just graduating from Bedford College in Cambridge with a Degree in Physics became the first elected woman president of the National Union of Students. At the headquarters in Bloomsbury she was soon busy organising various schemes that used students for voluntary vacation work of national importance.

Pilcher Research Rooms and Oliver Dining Hall.

The Main Entrance.

N Science across the Quadrangle.

Bomb Crater in the Grounds outside Tuke Building.

EDUCATING WOMEN

RETURNING 1944–46

Decisions about Returning

The College came back to Regent's Park for the session 1944-45 to buildings which three generations of students had never seen. Conditions were difficult and made worse by flying-bomb attacks which coincided with the period of return and caused superficial damage to various buildings.

There was much discussion as to whether this was a sensible time to return from Cambridge. In addition, as one third of the buildings were destroyed some staff and students argued that this was, perhaps, the right time for the College to move out from the centre of London. As we know, the College returned and re-built in Regent's Park.

Finding Space

Space had to be found to house all those Departments, services and individuals whose buildings had been destroyed. Tuke Building, South Science and Residence were packed to capacity. Services such as hot water had to be restored and there was a temporary boiler house in the ruins of N Science. Administration was housed in the ground floor of the residence. The Large Oliver Common Room was used first for food service and later for Council and other meetings. The catering and dining room service was nicknamed 'HMS Insatiable' and did wonders in its temporary quarters.

The search for extra buildings led College to many properties around the area of the park. Sussex Lodge, a villa in the Outer Circle was taken on a short lease to provide accommodation from 1944 to 1952 for the Departments from N Science: Botany, Geology and Zoology. There, away across the lake, an era of

The Ruins of the Administration Building from the Quadrangle 1946.

Sussex Lodge.

Canteen Ladies on the Library Steps 1947.

Emergency Canteen, Room 99 Tuke, 1939-47.

College science was conducted in cramped and dilapidated elegance. By arrangement with the Institute of Archaeology, the Departments of English and Classics were housed at St John's Lodge for 1944-46.

The Holme was leased from January, 1946. It was near to the College in the Inner Circle and the four acres of grounds stretched down to the lake. The lower floors were used for the Departments of English, Classics and Italian and the second floor became an extension of the College residence. Hanover Lodge in the Outer Circle was leased in 1947 and was immediately converted in to a residence for 30 students. Six houses in Broadhurst Gardens, NW6, were rented from 1945-49 as a residence.

College Colours

With the tennis team of 1946, in the centre of the front row, is Monica Cole who was later Professor of Geography in the College. This is one of the first photographs we have of blazers in the new College colours that had been adopted by the College Union Society after lengthy discussion at General meetings in the summer term of 1938. The Report of Council 1937-38 states 'At the request of the students the College colours are to be changed by adding the University colour of purple to the existing colours of silver and green'.

The colours of green, purple and silver-white were the colours of the Women's Social and Political Union. That colour scheme is attributed to Emmeline Pettick Lawrence, the Treasurer of the WSP Union and was in use during the militant campaigns for the vote in the decade preceding the First World War. The white stood for purity, green variously for hope, life and liberty, and purple for dignity, loyalty or royalty. Many people in the decades after 1940 believed that the College had planned for its colours to be the same as those of the feminist cause but we have found nothing to confirm this.

Magazines and Men

In 1946, after a break since 1941, the Bedford College Union Magazine was revived mainly as a literary magazine and so continued to 1965. It was given the main title of *The Unicorn*. The editorial in 1946 tells us that this title was second choice to *The Phoenix* referring to 'reiterated death and re-birth' of the magazine, but that title was already in use by Imperial College. The ideas behind the title *The Unicorn* were not explained.

There was also a news-sheet *Bedford News* 1946-61 and its successor *Inner Circular* 1962-82 and finally *The Absorber* 1981-85.

In 1946 a prefabricated hut was erected beside the Residence Drive near the hard tennis courts, it housed the Student Union Committee and Common Rooms. Also in 1946, the Council decided to admit men as registered postgraduate students. A few male research workers had been based in College since 1934 and Council indicated that an increase in applications from men to undertake research in College led to the change in policy. In the first year there were six male postgraduates in chemistry, three in physics and one in zoology. Council did not treat the change as momentous, it was buried in the middle of their Annual Report. However, it was thought by some people that these registered postgraduates were 'the thin end of the wedge' as far as admitting male undergraduates was concerned.

The Holme, Front Entrance.

Tennis Team 1946.

St John's Lodge.

EDUCATING WOMEN

RECONSTRUCTION 1947, 1948 AND 1949

The Architects

By the March of 1945 plans for the re-building of the ruined portions of College were complete and work started on the Oliver Building in April, 1947. Writing in 'The Builder' in January, 1953 when all was completed, the architects, Maxwell Ayrton and Partners noted 'From the commencement, in spite of the difficulties of the period both in labour and materials, it was determined that the quality of the works throughout should be the highest pre-war standard in workmanship and materials. It is pleasant to record that this was accomplished in every branch, everyone working together to that end with only one thought – that of the job as a whole – and was accomplished with rare harmony and happiness, a spirit largely born from that of the College authorities and staff ....'

Naming Buildings

At this time the Council took the important decision to re-name some of the surviving buildings as well as finding names for the new ones. Bedford College House in Swiss Cottage became Lindsell Hall. In Regent's Park, the S Science Block was to be called 'Arthur Acland' after the Rt Hon Sir A D Acland, Chairman of Council 1903–13. The College Residence was re-named Reid Hall, with Shaen, Bostock and Oliver Wings. It was the previous Reid Wing, or Reid Hall, which became the Bostock Wing after Eliza Bostock. In 1947 the very new 'Bedford News' started a series on Bedford Personalities with No 1 Reid Hall Cats.

Oliver

The new Oliver that replaced the tall, galleried Oliver Dining Hall, was of two storeys. The ground floor contained the kitchens and the Refectory and was ready for use in 1948; across a corridor were the two oak-panelled Common Rooms which had survived the bombing. The upper storey provided rooms for the Department of Mathematics and the building was completed in February, 1949.

Oliver Building, the Old Southern End and New Refectory Block.

Constructing the New Oliver Building 1947.

68

RECONSTRUCTION 1947, 1948 AND 1949

Herringham

Herringham Building was to replace the old Arts and Administration Block and work started in May, 1948. The photograph shows the builder's huts in the quadrangle, beyond them the Tuke Building with the Observatory and to the right are the chimneys of the temporary boiler house in the remains of N Science Block.

Preparations for the Centenary Celebrations

The Centenary of the Founding of the College was to be celebrated in 1949 whilst the reconstruction was underway. As after the first world war there was again a sudden increase in student numbers from the wartime low of 465 in 1939-40 to 680 in 1945-46 and now to 836 in 1948-49 of which 60 were postgraduates. The increase in numbers added to problems of accommodation, there were 19 academic Departments in 1949, one third of the students were in residence.

That the Centenary was well covered in the Press was helped perhaps by a little forethought. The President of the Student Union wrote in Bedford News in November, 1948, 'The topical subject best known to most people at the time of writing is that of our Centenary Plans .... most of my recent daily correspondence has been concerned with mascots and rag-processions. The Union Committee has decided that it does not wish to organise or sponsor a rag-procession. A picture of other Colleges .... mascots .... unruly fashion .... a straggly procession .... noisy fun .... hold up the traffic, suggests that the reporters of the more emphatic journals may be delighted, but that they might outheadline the more dignified and desirable Centenary Celebration reports'. Suggestions for a mascot included, amongst many others, a unicorn.

Oliver Refectory with High Table at the Northern End.

The Construction of Herringham 1948.

Construction of Herringham viewed from Tuke.

The Centenary Dinner 18th May, 1949 in the Oliver Refectory.

69

EDUCATING WOMEN

CENTENARY 1949, HERRINGHAM 1951

The Centenary

The Celebration of the 100 years since the founding of the College in 1849 started with a formal Dinner in the new refectory the previous evening but the main events were on Thursday, 19th May, 1949. In the morning there was a Thanksgiving Service at Marylebone Parish Church. In the afternoon the Official Assembly was held in College and HM Queen Mary joined the party; her car is seen here arriving at the garden side of Tuke Building.

After the assembly and speeches in Tuke Hall, the exhibitions in the science departments and the observatory and a tour of the grounds, Queen Mary took tea in the Senior Common Room. She completed her visit by attending the first performance of the Centenary Play given in Tuke Hall.

The Centenary Play had as its theme a discussion in the Elyssian Fields between a contemporary journalist knocked down on her way to the celebrations and John Stuart Mill, Mrs Reid, Miss Julia Smith (a member of the first College Council) and her niece Florence Nightingale. The dialogue centred on the difference between the lives of young women in 1949 and in the previous century.

Present and past members of staff worked on the play which was written and produced by Miss M St Clare Byrne who had been on the staff of the Department of English.

The Celebrations continued through the week with present students and friends having an open-day and a thousand-guest Centenary Ball on the Friday. Past students had a reception on the Saturday evening, the Union Society had a luncheon for representatives of other London Student Unions and finally the Council recorded its appreciation and gratitude to all who had contributed to this grand Centenary Celebration.

Herringham Building

Named for Sir Wilmot Herringham, Chairman of Council 1920–36 and benefactor of the College, Herringham Building was ready for occupation in January, 1951.

To the right of the main entrance was Herringham Hall which replaced 'The Large' of former years. The lofty height, the stage and the absence of fixed seating made it suitable for all sorts of College functions from formal lectures to

Arrival of Queen Mary 19th May 1949.

Centenary Tour of the Grounds Queen Mary is accompanied by the Principal, Miss G E M Jebb, and the Visitor of the College, Lord Macmillan.

The Centenary Play.

CENTENARY 1949, HERRINGHAM 1951

Freshers' Receptions. The audience gathered here for the traditional College teas before public lectures given in Tuke Hall. The list of uses was extended in later years when the stage was removed leaving a greater floor area for badminton, conferences and exhibitions.

The staircases, their walls decorated with pictures by Lady Christiana Herringham, led to College offices and the Council Room on the first floor and the Departments of Dutch, Greek and Latin on the top floor.

The library Periodicals Room was on the ground floor to the left of the main entrance. The view is of the room in use just after completion in 1952. Despite provision of the extra floor dividing Tate Library in 1932, there was now again much pressure for space within the library and this was a small welcome expansion. In later years, after further library extensions, this room became a stationery store and photocopying room.

Student Societies

Since the war the Student Societies had not reported regularly in the news-sheet. Instead they relied for attracting participation on the Student Handbook, the Freshers' Reception and the notice boards in the area of Reid and the Union Hut.

In the 1950s there were at least 24 Societies under the Student Union. The majority had subject allegiance but 4 were cultural, 4 political and 5 religious. There were in addition 18 Societies under the Athletic Union.

The Herringham Building and Main Entrance 1951.

The Periodicals Room in Herringham.

Staff Tennis Team 1950.

Herringham Hall.

EDUCATING WOMEN

CELEBRATIONS AND SCHOLARSHIP 1952

Darwin Building
The last of the new buildings was started in 1950, N Science was replaced by Darwin Building named for Major Leonard Darwin, Chairman of Council, 1913–20. In July, 1952 Darwin Building was ready for use by the Departments of Geology, Botany and Zoology. In the picture a practical class is in progress in the large teaching laboratory of the Department of Zoology on the top floor. The laboratory benches, fitted cupboards and floors in Darwin were of fine African hardwoods and post-war ideas for the planning of laboratories and lecture rooms were tentatively applied.

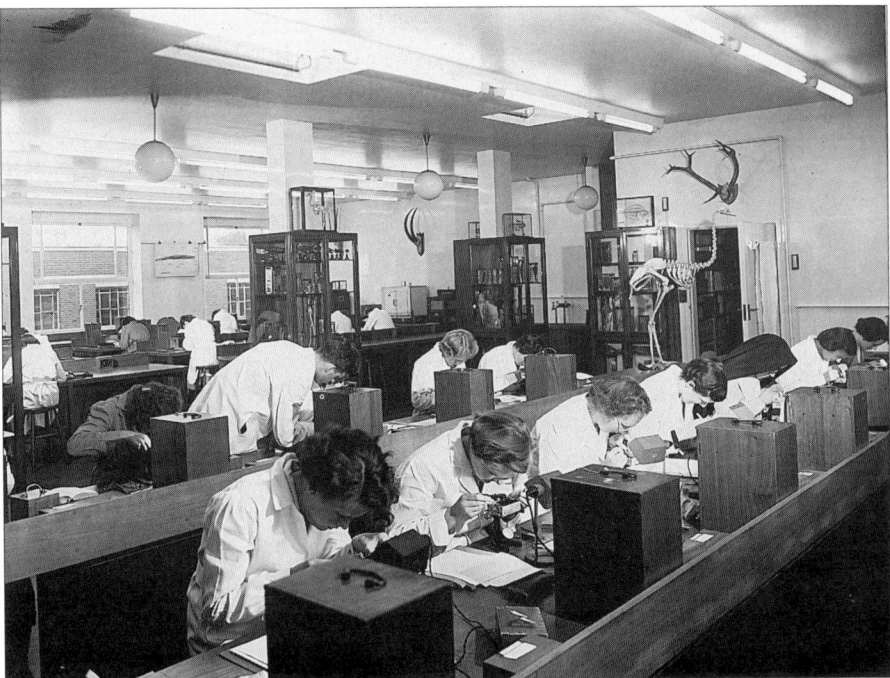
In the Zoology Laboratory.

Demolition of N Science Autumn 1949.

The Reconstruction Celebrations
Through the years HRH Princess Alice, wife of the Chancellor of London University, the Earl of Athlone, performed many services for Bedford College and happily she and her husband presided at the Reconstruction Celebrations on 28th October, 1952. The official party also included the Chairman of Council, Sir Charles Tennyson, Dame Lilian Penson, the ex-Principal Miss Jebb, Principal Dr Norah Penston, and the President of the Student Union.

Extract from the editorial of the Bedford News, November, 1952, by Jean Rook.

'At the Reconstruction Celebrations on October 28 the spirit which is diffused through so many separate associations was concentrated in one place at last. In Tuke Hall on that day there was not only the College as it is at present, but also the College which had struggled through the "lean years" and by doing so had made possible the great occasion in which we were now privileged to take part.

'Those who were at the Celebrations saw and felt the strength of Bedford College as a united body. We saw it in the brilliant tableau on the platform and in the flock of black gowns fluttering in the quadrangle, and we felt it in the subdued excitement just before the ceremony began and in the mounting applause which greeted the Principal when she rose to speak. We realised then that the bonds which bind us together are not less strong because they are not always visible.'

Scholarship
From 1948–51 Professor Lilian Penson was Vice-Chancellor of the University of London, the first woman to hold such a position in this country. In 1951 the King awarded her the DBE for services to education. She had a long and exceptionally distinguished period of service with the College from her appointment in 1930 to the Chair of

The Opening Ceremony on Herringham Terrace. Reconstruction Celebrations.

CELEBRATIONS AND SCHOLARSHIP 1952

Left to right: Dame Lilian Penson, HRH Princess Alice and the Principal, Dr Norah Penston.

Modern History until her retirement in 1962. Her publications in colonial and diplomatic history of the eighteenth and nineteenth centuries led on to work on the Commission on Higher Education in the Colonies and also on the Fulbright scheme.

Generations of students bear witness to her work as a teacher and her skill as a director of research. She held many offices and gave service in administration in both the University and the College and her scholarship and sense of public duty were recognised by the award of several Honorary Degrees and other distinctions.

Academic Staff
The official party at the Reconstruction Celebrations toured the new buildings. In the Botany Library in Darwin Building they were shown precious books, including the Redouté Lilies, by the Professor of Botany, Leslie Audus; the sketches of fellow academics on this page are his work.

Barbara Wooton.

Gladys Turquet.

Theodoor Weevers.

Lilian Penson.

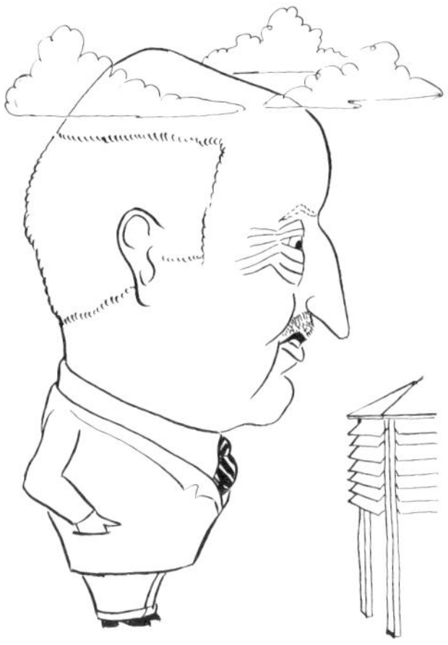

Gordon Manley.

In the Botany Library left to right: Miss G. Jebb, Prof L Audus and Dame Lilian Penson.

Leonard Hawkes.

73

EDUCATING WOMEN

THE 1950s

Adjusting the Space

After the post-war expansion, the early 1950s was a period of consolidation. Developments in teaching and research and the revision of Degree Courses called for additional staff and equipment and the College was able to meet these needs. By the mid 1950s more accommodation was required and so started the continual search for space which occupied the College Administration, with increasing frustration, through to the 1980s. Galleries and mezzanine floors were added in Acland Building. The Pilcher Wing built in the space between Oliver and Herringham provided new areas for some Arts Departments.

In 1958–59 an extension was made between the two wings of Reid Hall. This gave more study bedrooms and bathrooms on the upper floors and Common Room and other space for the Student Union on the ground floor. The prefabricated hut beside the Residence Drive, which had housed the Student Union since 1946, was then removed. A new wing and extra storey were added to Tuke Building providing for some science departments.

In 1959 the College acquired a long lease of St John's Lodge, another Regency Villa in the Inner Circle just beyond the Holme and reinstatement of the premises was complete in 1962. At first it provided residential and Union accommodation and later for the Departments of History, Greek and Latin. The Ballroom will be recalled by generations of examination candidates.

The Staff

Mr Harold Chipperton, the Head Gardener, retired in 1954 after 43 years of service to the College. In the group gathered at his retirement party are technical staff, gardeners, maintenance men, engineers, carpenters and refectory staff. The group is pictured outside Mr Chipperton's home in the Lodge on the Library Drive.

Aerial View mid 1950s.

The Reid Hall Infill.

Hustings 1955 Bedford News.

THE 1950s

Student Activities

In 1952 the College opened a shop where stationery and instruments were available at reasonable prices; it was taken over by the Student Union in 1965. To mark the coronation of HM Queen Elizabeth in 1953 there was an Open-day Garden Party hosted by the students, the purchase of a television set for the Student Common Room and a subsidy for the Coronation Ball. Dances were regular events whether Society Hops or Union Balls.

The Boat Club used a legacy to buy a second boat, a pair-oar, which was launched on the lake in Regent's Park to be used for training and practising. The main activities of the Club were now no longer on the Park lake.

In 1956, when the BC Union Magazine had been entitled *The Unicorn* for ten years, the students decided that a model of a unicorn should replace the belisha beacon

Lacrosse Team 1951.

in Tuke Hall and 10 of its 45 players were from Bedford College. Inter-collegiate events included Fashion Show competitions and the very successful 'Concours Dramatique' in which the students of the French Department won the cup in 1958.

Fashion Shows were popular; in 1958 the Unicorn was regained by Bedford students from marauders at Imperial College by dazzling them with a requested 'Fashion Show' into relinquishing their prize. A series of staff-student teas was started in College with the aim of better communications but they did not flourish for long. A number of open-days were held over these years and

in March, 1958, the Union organised an evening Conversazione 'Bedford at Home' which attracted 700 guests to see exhibitions and displays put on by the students and departments.

Renovating the Telescope

The Telescope had deteriorated during the war particularly because of the idle games of the fire-watchers in the roof-top Observatory. It needed renovation and skilled re-setting before it could be used again. This work was carried out by Vic Little and Frank Grimes of the Physics Department so that the Observatory and the Telescope again became a part of College life.

The Unicorn Regained from Imperial College.

'Arabella' as the College mascot. At a party at the London Zoo a white kid was formally adopted as a live representation for the Unicorn.

New premises for the University of London Union, ULU, were opened in Malet Street and more student activities began to centre there. In May, 1955, the University of London Orchestra gave its foundation concert

'Our Other Unicorn' Bedford News.

Mr Chipperton's Retirement Party 1954.

EDUCATING WOMEN

ROBBINS AND MEN 1963–67

Difficult Expansion

The Robbins Report of 1963 paved the way for a three-fold expansion of University Education which twenty years later had to be painfully retracted. The response to Robbins in Bedford College meshed in with actions that had been discussed over the years in Development Plans and resulted in a number of changes.

* A 40% increase in undergraduate numbers to 1,200 by 1966 and 1,500+ student places planned by 1972.
* The admission of men undergraduates without reduction in places for women.
* The institution of more new Degree subjects and combinations.
* The adoption by the Science Faculty of Course-Unit Degrees.

The increase in numbers led to many more changes in the use of space and transfers of accommodation. Every part of the College was involved: academic departments, registry, library, Student Union, refectory, residences and sports ground. Over-crowding was a real problem and supporting services were severely taxed. The Maintenance Department had in its care buildings which were now 50 years old. The effects of war-time bombs still showed and facilities such as the electricity supply and boilers needed modernization. Repairs and adaptations were fitted in to the schedule for new building. Forays for planning permission and the noise of pneumatic drills accompanied the academic advances.

Departmental Changes

In 1962–64 the original Wernher Reading Room was demolished and in its place the new three-storey Jebb Building provided extensions for the Department of Physiology and the Library The entrance to the new Wernher Reading Room gave access to the rest of the Library. There was now a second Reading Room named after Agnes Paterson, a former Librarian who was killed in London by enemy action during the war. The library had 45% more floor space and the periodicals were transferred back to the main library which now had a total of nearly 137,000 volumes.

The Botany Garden Laboratories were built in 1965–66 as an extension around the Sargent Laboratory in the Botany Garden. They provided teaching and research space including a greenhouse-laboratory specially

Entrance to the New Wernher Reading Room.

The Botany Garden Laboratories.

BLOG, some of the Cast of Trial by Jury *1967.*

designed for radioactive work with plants.

Other changes for academic departments in the next few years included the moves of Dutch, German, Philosophy, Greek, Latin and Sociology to Reid Hall on the departure of the last student residents from the main site. The Department of History moved in to St John's Lodge and Geography and Zoology made use of the Bedford College Annexe created in the former Arthur Stanley Institute in Peto Place.

Male Undergraduates

Discussions, arguments and sometimes bitter skirmishes preceded the decision to admit male undergraduates who were registered for the first time in October, 1965. Our pictures show some of the consequences of that decision.

BLOG was Bedford Light Opera Group whose annual productions cheered each Lent Term in College. The whole enterprise was inspired by Bill Bishop who joined the staff of the Department of Geology in 1965 and is seen at the extreme left in the line-up of the cast of the first production *Trial by Jury* in 1967. BLOG helpers did wonders each year to transform Tuke Hall and its stage for the very polished productions which soon had substantial orchestral backing under the direction of Barry Hall. In 1974 Bill Bishop moved to Queen Mary College and as Dora Smee noted at that time 'Everyone enjoyed the productions, an oasis in Bedford as the Dramatic Society had passed out. It must be tremendous satisfaction to him to know how much he did for the College and for the students. So many students must have made abiding friendships'. The unexpected and untimely death of Bill Bishop in 1977 was marked by a BLOG production *Memories are Made of This*. In College, Light Opera productions continued through to 1985.

Wednesday afternoons had long been the time when sports teams from the different Colleges were free to play against one another. From 1965 there were football teams waiting in Herringham on Wednesday lunchtimes for their bus to take them to a match. Training sessions were held twice a week nearer home. By 1967–68 Bedford were in action in the University Cup Final which they narrowly lost. The Bedford teams were lucky to be trained by Frank Grimes, Chief Technician in the Physics Workshop and a qualified FA coach. He is seen here in the front row with the 1972–73 Team.

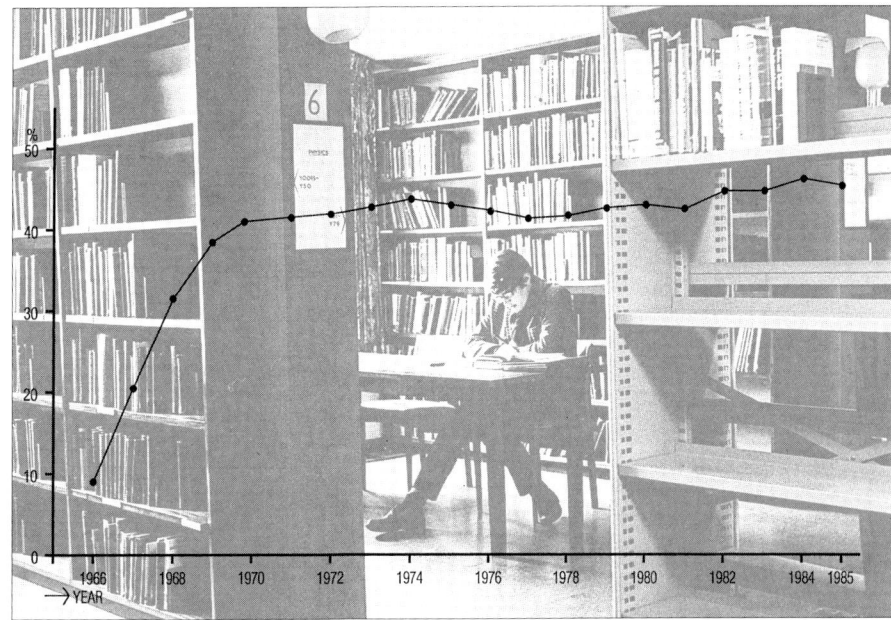
Male Students as a Percentage of Total Students.

The 1972–73 Football Team outside Tuke.

The 1967–68 Cup Final at Motspur Park.

EDUCATING WOMEN

SCR AND FELLOWS 1965–69

Prefabrication

In 1967 and 1970 the pressure on space in the College resulted once again in the use of prefabricated buildings. The Army Huts of 1919 and 1946 were recalled when in 1967 a prefabricated building was erected in the quadrangle to provide teaching and office space for the Departments of Physics and Chemistry. In 1970 the link with the University Computer was re-located in a prefabricated building set in the well of the south-eastern extension of Tuke Building.

The Holme

The elegant villa and its grounds were much appreciated not only by those who studied there but also for the annual summer gatherings of College groups. The resident students enjoyed the early morning, lakeside views of nesting herons or grazing goslings until the Holme was no longer used for residence from 1975.

The Quadrangle filled with Prefabricated Building 1967–84.

Staff Association Summer Party at the Holme.

SCR AND FELLOWS 1965-69

Fellows

In 1926 the Council instituted the office of Fellow of the College. The first Fellow was Sir Hildred Carlile under the classification of 'eminent persons who have rendered signal service to the College'.

Kathleen Lonsdale DBE, FRS, DSc, (1903–1971) graduated from Bedford College with a Degree in Physics in 1922. She became Professor of Chemistry in the University of London, Head of the Department of Crystallography at University College and is seen here signing the Fellows Book after her appointment as Fellow in 1965.

Dame Kathleen was the finest X-ray crystallographer of her generation, one of the first two women to be elected to the Royal Society in 1945 and fifteen years later she became its Vice-President. She was Professor at University College 1949–68 and in 1968 the first woman President of the British Association for the Advancement of Science. She was a worker for peace and in that cause, having refused to register for Civil Defence Duties, she spent a month in prison in the Second World War.

Staff Association

Bedford College Staff Association was founded in 1917 and organised the Senior Common Room and a varying programme of social events. The Senior Common Room was on the ground floor of the north wing of Tuke Building. Social events included the Christmas celebration and for a fair number of years this was a formal dinner with entertainment. There was also a farewell end-of-session summer party held on the terrace of the Holme overlooking the lake.

The Refectory

The refectory changed its style. It no longer provided for resident students and resident vacation conferences. The wooden tables, High Table and the dais disappeared and food service was geared to selection at the servery and snack bars. In 1967–69 there was a major rebuilding of the kitchens to help cope with the new ways. The Refectory and the Union Coffee bar in Reid both came under pressure from the increased student numbers.

Dame Kathleen Lonsdale signing the Fellows Book: with Chairman of Council, Dame Mary Smieton, and on the extreme right the Principal, Mrs Sally Chilver.

The Senior Common Room.

Oliver Refectory.

EDUCATING WOMEN

HANOVER LODGE AND TENNYSON HALL

1947–1962

The original Villa of Hanover Lodge was built probably about 1827 but substantially altered before this view was taken from the eastern side. It stood in five acres of grounds and in 1947 was adapted to provide accommodation for thirty residents. Hanover Lodge was in the Outer Circle about 15 minutes' walk across the park from College.

1965–1985

A long-term building lease was obtained and though it was a difficult canal-side site plans were approved and the new Wings and Dining Hall were built during 1962–65. The new Hall of Residence with single study bedrooms for 231 women students was in full operation for the 1966–67 session and it was formally opened by HM Queen Elizabeth The Queen Mother in June, 1967. From 1970 the Hall was available to both men and women students. Because of the heavy demand for residence, the policy was to allow students two out of their three undergraduate years in a residence.

1970

The anonymous benefactor who had given to Colleges of the University of London more than £3,500,000 in the past nine years, offered in 1970 to provide £300,000 for a new hall of residence for men and women students at Bedford College. It proved impossible to find a suitable site though the idea of further development at Hanover Lodge was investigated. Finally the offer could not be accepted.

Hanover Lodge, The Villa.

The Old House and the New Wings 1966.

A Student's Room.

The Entrance to Hanover Lodge 1966.

HANOVER LODGE AND TENNYSON HALL

Tennyson Hall

The leases of Nos 10, 11 and 12 Dorset Square were acquired in 1966 and after alterations Tennyson Hall opened for 50 men students at Easter, 1968.

Sir Charles Tennyson, Chairman of the College Council 1946-53, is seen on the extreme right here arriving for the opening ceremonies of the Hall. Welcoming him are the Senior Resident Student on the left and in the centre Les Turnbull, Warden of the Hall.

From 1955, Les Turnbull was a Lecturer in the Department of Botany and from 1967, Registrar of the College. Before establishing Tennyson Hall he had been on the staff of Commonwealth Hall one of the University Halls of Residence for students from all of the London Colleges.

'Crisis in Students' Lodgings' was a frequent press headline during the post-Robbins expansion of the late 1960s. This crisis was reduced somewhat for Bedford's students by the new Tennyson Hall and the extended Hanover Lodge both of which were only a short walk from the Garden Gate of the College.

The Garden Gate

This was previously known as the Little Gate and it led to the bridge over the park lake, past the flower beds and to the Outer Circle and Baker Street, a walk well-known to most members of the College.

Nottingham Place – Rachel Notcutt Hall

Lindsell Hall and Hanover Lodge both became mixed-sex Halls whilst Tennyson Hall was solely for men. The Hall reserved for women was Nottingham Place, later named Rachel Notcutt Hall to commemorate both Rachel Notcutt and Notcutt House.

The North side of Dorset Square, Tennyson Hall.

Arriving for the Opening Ceremonies of Tennyson Hall.

RESIDENCES FOR STUDENTS OF BEDFORD COLLEGE Years in existence and (number of students)		
The Home, 6 Grenville St, Brunswick Sq, WC1	1852–1861	(9–13)
The Boarding House, 48 Bedford Sq, WC1	1861–1874	(13–20)
York Place, Baker Street, NW1	1874–1915	(40)
South Villa, Bedford College, NW1	1909–1930	(16)
Shaen Hall and Reid Hall, Bedford College, NW1	1913–1966	(90)
Notcutt House, Dorset Sq, NW1	1915–1941	(60)
Bedford College House, Lindsell Hall, NW3	1919–1982	(37–100)
The Hostel, Fitzjohns Ave, NW3	1944–1945	(38)
The Holme (2nd Floor) Bedford College, NW1	1945–1975	(9–11)
15–25 Broadhurst Gardens, NW6	1945–1949	(60)
Hanover Lodge, Outer Circle, Regent's Park, NW1	1947–1985	(30–240)
Rachel Notcutt Hall, (44) 17 Nottingham Place, W1	1951–1984	(16–22)
11, Wedderburn Road, NW3	1962–1972	(16)
St John's Lodge (postgraduates), Bedford College, NW1	1962–1965	(5)
Tennyson Hall, Dorset Sq, NW1	1968–1985	(51)

The Name Board at the Garden Gate.

EDUCATING WOMEN

LINDSELL HALL. DEGREES AWARDED

Adamson Road Hostel – Bedford College House

Contributions collected from former students in 1919 enabled the College to purchase three houses in Adamson Road, Swiss Cottage, to hold 37 residents. Three further houses were added by 1925 and with 78 students in residence the group was then named Bedford College House, BCH.

By 1928, as a result of further purchases and some sales, the College had the freehold of six adjacent houses in Adamson Road and the leasehold of one house in Buckland Crescent across the joined garden. On the Adamson Road site, communication-ways were made to join the six houses, heating and hot water systems were centrally installed and many large rooms divided. The large Dining Room and Common Room were created by building out on some of the garden.

The extended BCH was home to generations of students under the care of Miss Alice Lindsell who was Warden from 1919–38. The Hall paid its way during these years and was well-equipped and free from outside debt. As in each of the three main College residences at this time, the students at BCH organised in-house events and developed their own traditions. The picture shows some of the residents of BCH at the last Saturday evening dance of the summer term 1932–33.

Lindsell Hall

The Council decided in 1944 to rename the residence Lindsell Hall. During the war it had housed a 'British Restaurant' available to the local population, a refuge for bombed-out Londoners and an ARP post.

Few structural changes had been made to the houses since the 1930s and so eventually alterations were urgently needed to provide extra bathrooms and a fireproof stairway. These were provided in 1972 when a glass and metal-framed infill was built in a gap between two blocks of the Adamson Road houses. In 1968–69 the Hall held 87 students, all women, but in 1969–70 men students were housed in Buckland. Lindsell Hall thus became the first College 'mixed' Hall of Residence. From 1968 to 1978 Lindsell maintained its tradition of Guest Night Dinners to which members of the College staff were invited by their students, a very pleasant inter-disciplinary social event.

The Garden and Buckland 1978.

Saturday-evening Dance 1933.

Lindsell Hall, Adamson Road, frontage post-1972.

LINDSELL HALL. DEGREES AWARDED

DEGREES OF THE UNIVERSITY OF LONDON AWARDED TO STUDENTS OF BEDFORD COLLEGE
(EXCLUDING D.Sc. and D Litt.)

Degrees of the University of London are not the only qualifications for which the College has prepared students. In the 1880s, after training at Bedford College some students continued to Oxford or Cambridge in order to complete their Degrees. Other qualifications for which Bedford College trained students are listed.

From the College
  Associates Diploma
  Hygiene Certificate/Diploma
  Health Visitors Diploma
  Social Studies Certificate
  Training Department Certificate
  Diploma in Pedagogy
  Diploma in Sociology
  Diploma in Social Studies
  Diploma in Applied Social Studies
  Diploma in Advanced Chemistry
  Diploma in Nuclear Physics

From the University of London
  Preliminary Scientific
  Matriculation
  Intermediate in Medicine
  First and Second MB
  Teachers Diploma
  Diploma for Journalism
  Academic Diploma in Biology
  Academic Diploma in Geography
  Academic Diploma in Psychology
  Academic Diploma in Sociology
  Diploma in Applied Social Studies

From other authorities
  Cambridge Teachers Diploma
  Cambridge University Higher Local
  Sanitary Inspectors Examination Board
  Sanitary Institute Inspector of Nuisances

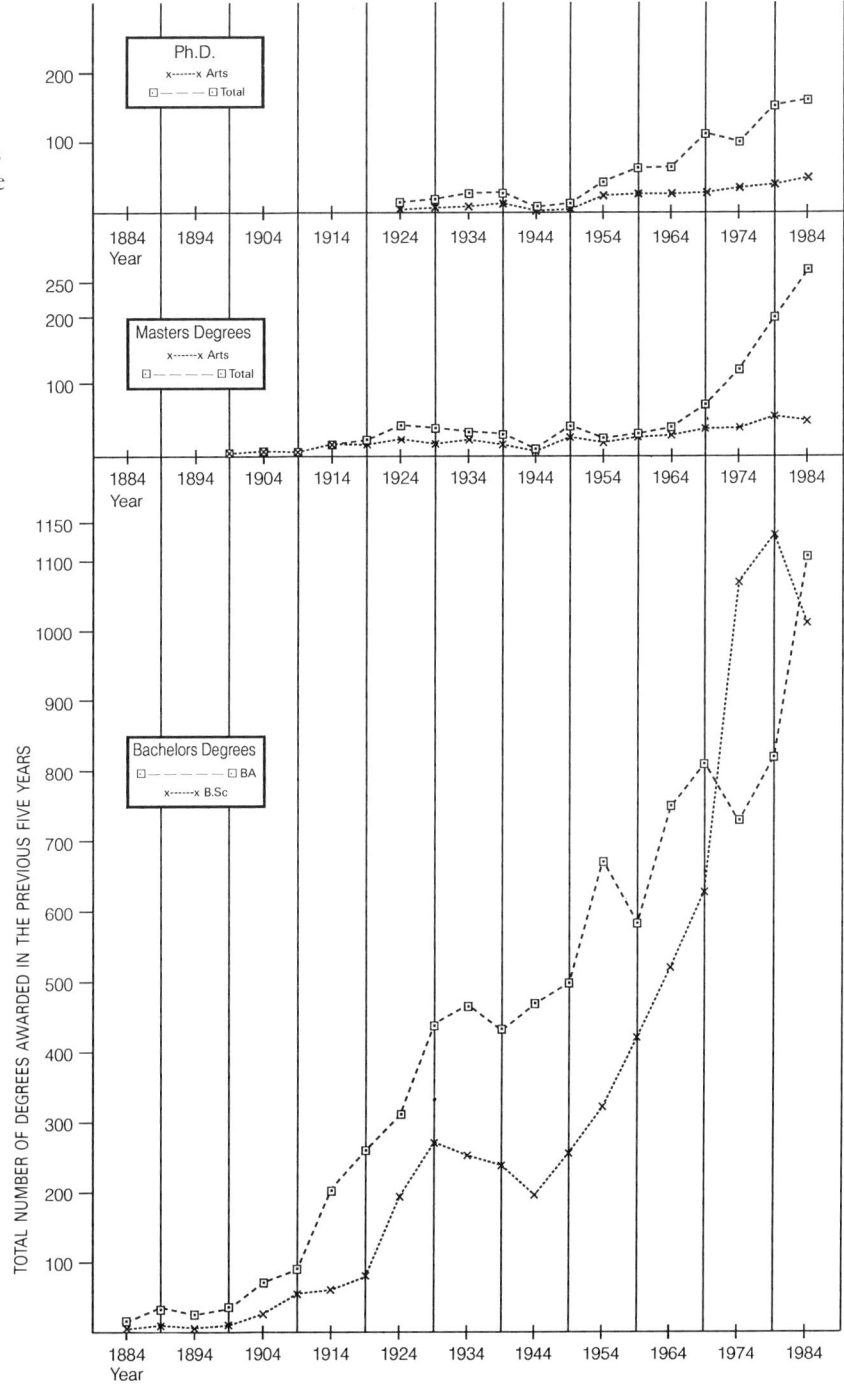

Physics Laboratory 1968.

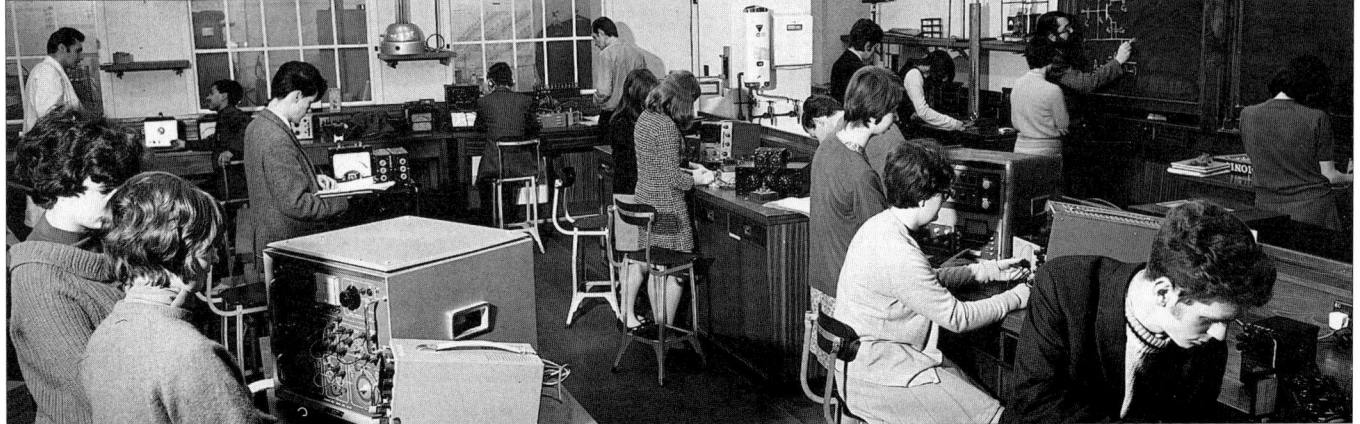

83

EDUCATING WOMEN

THE 1970s

Student Protest

The late 60s and early 70s were memorable for student protest actions in many parts of the world. Protests focussed on a variety of political and local causes and were sometimes quiet and reasoned, sometimes disruptive and sometimes violent. Bedford College was not immune. There were sit-ins and in 1970 an occupation of the administration offices over the question of 'secret' or 'political' files. In the same year a subsequent referendum in the Union showed that the majority of students were against such action. A few students adopted the policy of spraying slogans on doors and walls in College, causing minor but disruptive damage.

A series of discussion meetings for the whole of the College were instituted. At the time of the sit-in they attracted 800 people but later only a few dozen attended and they soon ceased. In the same year as the sit-in moves began for the greater participation of students in the committee structure of the College and students appeared in attendance at meetings of the Council.

A Centenarian

When Miss Edith Ellen Humphrey celebrated her 100th birthday in September, 1975, by planting a tree at her home in Highgate, North London, she reckoned she was the world's oldest woman scientist. From the North London Collegiate School she entered Bedford College in 1893 having won a College Pfeiffer Science Scholarship. She was active in students affairs but must have worked hard in the new laboratories for she gained further

Bedford Students in Baker Street, NUS Day of Action 1971.
(Picture by Times Educational Supplement)

College scholarships to support herself and graduated in 1897 with Honours in Physics and Chemistry. She went straight on to study in Zurich and the magazine back home in College noted that 'She is engaged upon a "Doktor-Arbeit" on a compound of cobalt. We feel it would perhaps be an excellent thing if we were required to sign a document promising diligence in study, as she was at Zurich University'.

Miss Humphrey became the first female assistant to the Professor, Mendeleev, who was the proponent of the periodic table of the elements and one of the founding fathers of chemistry. She gained her doctorate in 1901 with a double distinction, an honour given only once previously.

Speaking in 1975, Miss Humphrey said 'I did chemistry just because I like it, that was where things were happening'. She is pictured at the tree-planting celebrations.

Sport

The student Athletic Union ceased to exist as a separate body in 1969–70 and was replaced by a Sports Committee which was part of the Union Society, BCUS. In 1971 planning permission was finally refused for the erection of an inflatable sports hall on the tennis court at the Holme. Inter-departmental sporting conflict is watched in 1974 by the Principal, Dr John Black; a relay race between teams from Botany and Zoology is starting off outside Queen Mary's Rose Garden.

A Centenarian.   (Pictures by Hornsey Journal)

THE 1970s

Development

In the dozen or so years since the Robbins Report there had been substantial changes in the students and staff of the College. Some of these are summarised for us in an account in the BCA Journal, 1976, by Kathleen Spears who was a student of the College in the 1930s, associated with it in various capacities since and College Secretary 1962–76. 'Overall student numbers have increased by approximately two-thirds, undergraduates increasing by about a half and postgraduates by more than three-fold. Total staff numbers have grown in nearly the same overall proportions. An annual budget in 1962 of £485,463 has in 1975 become one of £2,717,630. The highest proportional increases in student numbers have been in science and the social sciences. The highest proportional staff increases have been in the numbers of research and technical support staff. Within the budget, expenditure on grant-aided research has risen from a mere £5,178 pa to £169,487 pa. Put rather more succinctly, the development of the College has been in the pure and social sciences and in postgraduate studies and research.'

More Infilling

One of the first problems encountered when work was started for the Tuke-Darwin Infill Building in 1971, was the tough old stable-yard foundations left from the days of South Villa. Underground springs and streams of water had often been troublesome in College foundations. The flow of these had altered slowly since 1911 because of changes in surrounding districts and they had to be investigated anew before each planned building.

Preparations for the Tuke-Darwin Infill.

Student Union Common Room, Ground Floor of Reid.

The Relay Race 1974.

EDUCATING WOMEN

THE LAST TEN YEARS

A Symbol for the Appeal adopted by the BCA Magazine.

1976 Football Club.

University of London Cup Final 1977.

Student Activities

The Student Union Bar of 1975 is in the original, oak-panelled Large Oliver Common Room now much more crowded than it was in 1913. This bar was in addition to the facilities in Reid Hall where BCUS and adjacent academic departments had an uneasy relationship in an overcrowded state. This was just one of the needs for more space. The BCUS Report of 1980–81 listed 33 Student Societies and 18 Sports Clubs and there were now three sabbatical officers in the Union.

The Football Club of 1976–77 met with most success winning the Premier League and Cup double. In 1977–78 the Club's first XI represented the University in the Amateur Football Association competition and won the trophy,

The Modernised Tate Reading Room. Library Stock in 1983–84 was 236,067 volumes.

A Student Union Bar in Oliver Common Room 1975.

THE LAST TEN YEARS

A Symbol for the Appeal.

Panorama of the College.

demonstrating they were the most consistent side in ULU over the past few seasons. The Frank Grimes Trophy was established in College for outstanding contributions to sport and was a tribute to his long and loyal service to College sport. Frank's wider contributions were recognised by the award to him of the Queen's Jubilee Medal in 1978.

Development Appeal

The Appeal was launched in 1978 with the aim of raising money for a number of new buildings and extensions. At first in the hands of professional fund-raisers, it gathered momentum when later taken over by the College. New fund-raising ventures were tried as well as old favourites. The students organised a sponsored netball marathon. There were Garden Fetes in 1980 and 1981 when most of the College departments joined in with money-making enterprises like that of the catering staff seen at the 1981 Fete.

An Appeal symbol was designed and used on merchandise and to publicise Appeal events. These included the Exhibition of 'The Regent's Park Villas and the People who Lived in Them' which was held at the Holme. Efforts were made to involve the College in the communities of St Marylebone and Camden. The panoramic view was taken at about this time and shows both the tightly packed College buildings and also the local communities crowding at the outskirts of the park.

Finance and Merger

As a result of the Appeal, the Wolfson Psychology Laboratory was built over the kitchens in the Oliver Block. This was the only building development before the combination of increases in costs with stand-stills and cut-backs in government funding, overshadowed all efforts at further development in Regent's Park. There was much discussion in College and widespread scrutiny of the finances. There were some fruitless explorations of the possibility of merging with various other Colleges of London University. Finally, amidst well-argued opposition, the decision was made to proceed to a merger with Royal Holloway College at Egham and the first academic departments moved there in 1982.

HM Queen Elizabeth the Queen Mother paid a farewell visit to the College at Regent's Park in May, 1984. The picture shows the Queen Mother speaking to the Student Union President, Miss Delyth Morgan, and accompanied by (left to right) The Vice Principal, Dr John Prebble, the Principal, Professor Dorothy Wedderburn, and the Chairman of Council Professor Sir Cyril Clarke.

Fund-raising Garden Fete 1981.

The Last Royal Visit 1984.

EDUCATING WOMEN

REUNION AND FAREWELL

The Last Session
About 600 students were on the Regent's Park site during the last session 1984-85, the rest had transferred to Egham. Acland and Reid Buildings were already being refurbished by the new tenant and teaching and other activities were re-located on the site; the Union Society operated from Oliver.

The Mixed Hockey Team 1984-85.

Gathering at Herringham Entrance.

The Reunion
The College Reunion was held on 15th June, 1985, and the seven views show how the College looked on that day. A bright sun shone on the thousands of former students who came to Regent's Park. They came to see again their College, to meet with teachers, mentors and cherished friends, to view the changes since their day and to ponder on the spirit that had developed in this College since 1849 and to ponder also on its future.

The College Flag was Flying on Tuke.

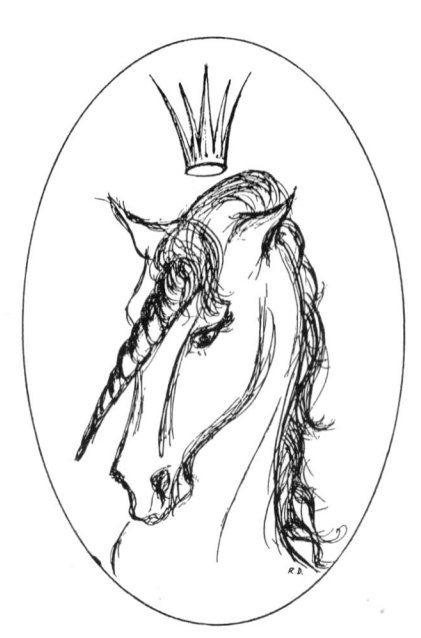

REUNION AND FAREWELL

Picnic Lunch Outside Tuke.

One of the Departmental Exhibitions: Geology.

The Exhibition of College History in Herringham Hall.

Herringham Terrace from the re-turfed Quadrangle.

The Archive Exhibition in the Council Room.

EDUCATING WOMEN

MOVING AND END WORD

Moving

In the early decades of Tuke Building, when ducks nested on its roof their ducklings reached the lake by going over the parapet and straight down to the ground. Now, in September, 1985, when the telescope was removed from the Observatory, it too went over the roof and straight down on the garden-side of Tuke Building. The telescope was taken to Egham where a new dome was built for it.

The practical move of the College to Egham was spread over the years 1982 to 1985, a daunting task for everyone involved. Two people much concerned with the move were Marigold Pakenham-Walsh who controlled arrangements for the moving and Elizabeth Bennett who collected, catalogued and moved the archives. At that very busy time they both gave support to the production of the Reuinion Exhibition in Herringham Hall. The author wishes to thank them for this and for their later encouragement in the production of this book. Thanks are due also to the last Council of Bedford College who gave their approval to both projects.

The Descent of the Telescope 1985.

END WORD

*by Dorothy Wedderburn Principal
Bedford College 1981–1985
Royal Holloway and Bedford New College 1985–1990*

Lord Scarman, when Chairman of the Court of London University, once described Bedford College as the jewel in its crown. The College could stake this claim not just because of its pioneering role in the development of higher education for women in the mid nineteenth century, nor just because of the intellectual stars who were associated with it – Susan Stebbing, Kathleen Lonsdale, Barbara Wotton to name but a few – but because of the steady stream of good quality graduates it produced over nearly a century and a half. But one of the most noteable features of Bedford was the great affection it generated among its staff and students. This charming memento recording pictorially the history of the College bears witness to this.

Many contributed to the organisation of the hugely successful reunion to say farewell to the Regent's park site before the final move to Egham to create the new college of Royal Holloway and Bedford. But none did more than Linna Bentley who has now produced this permanent record. Linna was herself a popular teacher of biology as well as a much loved warden of Lindsell Hall.

Reading this account, however reminds us that one of Bedford's outstanding characteristics was its ability to change. Including the wartime evacuation, it changed location no less than three times. So when the merger came and it was necessary to move out to Egham this was seen as one more, albeit major, upheaval. Today, with its fine new buildings added to the glory of Thomas Holloway's original edifice which formed Royal Holloway College, the new combined College has over three thousand students and as a beautiful campus within London University is increasingly popular. This popularity derives in part because the original strengths of its two founding colleges have been retained and enhanced. What the reader will see in these pages of the spirit of Bedford continues in Royal Holloway and Bedford New College as it faces the challenges of the nineties and beyond.

MOVING AND END WORD

Acknowledgements for support and for the use of photographs and other materials.

L D Adams, L J Audus
Bedford College Association, S Bell
E M Cannon, M Cole, R Coleman, P Cushway
R Dalby, H Davenport
J C Funnell, M Gascoyne, F Grimes, E W Gildersleeves
D Hall, Hornsey Journal, G Hopkins, M Harrop
M Jay, C Jenkinson, U K Johnson
E Lakeman, W A Leyshon
K Maslen, E V Mitchell, K Ostberg
G Page, M Parker, M E Payne, Z Podhorodecki, S Ponsford, L Roper
B Sharman, A Taylor, K Tillotson, Times Educational Supplement
E Vollans, P Wilson, A G Towers

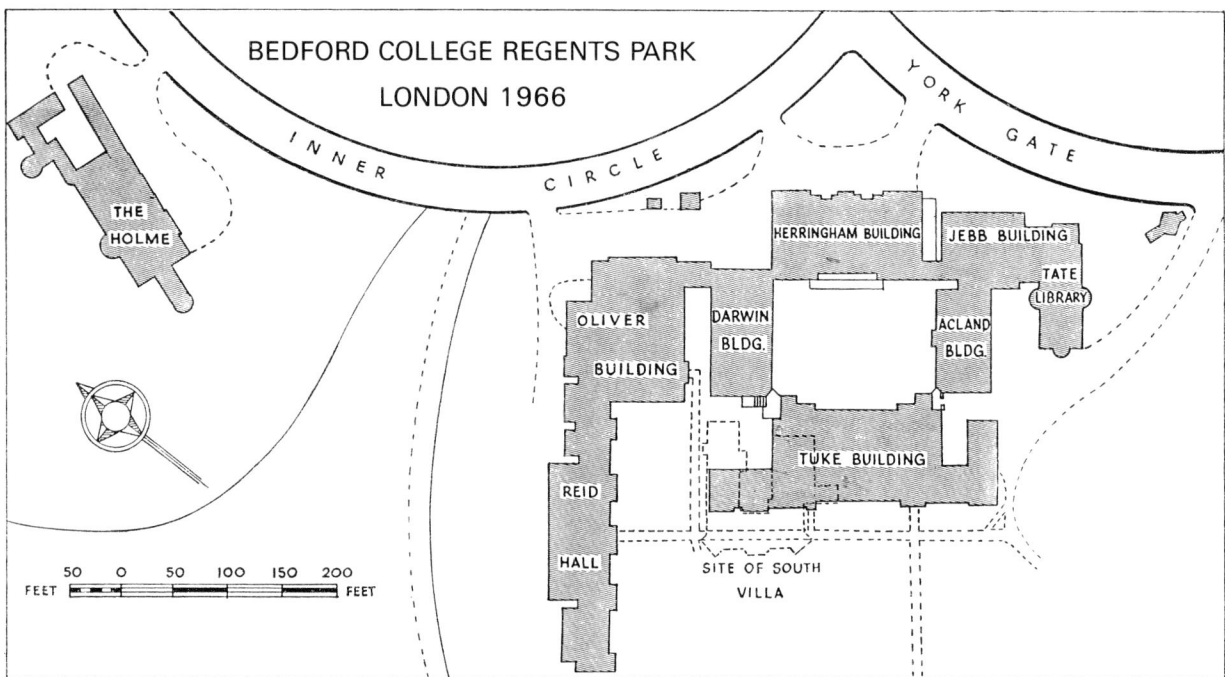

The publication of this book was assisted by Royal Holloway and Bedford New College with funds from the sale of the Florentine terracotta figure of the Angel Gabriel, c,1510, attributed to Benedetto Buglioni, which is pictured on pages 29 and 59.

Design & Origination
by Flaydemouse, Yeovil

Printed & Bound by
CASTLE CARY PRESS LTD.
CASTLE CARY
SOMERSET